Tales from

AMERICA'S VACATIONLAND

Tales from
AMERICA'S VACATIONLAND

Joe Delta

iUniverse, Inc.
Bloomington

TALES FROM AMERICA'S VACATIONLAND

iUniverse books may be ordered through booksellers or by contacting:

iUniverse
1663 Liberty Drive
Bloomington, IN 47403
www.iuniverse.com
1-800-Authors (1-800-288-4677)

ISBN: 978-1-4620-2462-9 (sc)
ISBN: 978-1-4620-2463-6 (ebk)

Printed in the United States of America

iUniverse rev. date: 07/06/2011

GREAT MEN?

Palm Beach, Florida in the later New Deal era (1947):

It was one of the many hot, humid and oppressive mornings in the tropics, the kind that makes you want to be someplace north of Sweden atop an icy fjord.

A devoted and doting Palm Beach grandmamma had concluded that she had had enough of little junior's fights, trespasses, vandalism and criminal behavior in general. He had outdone even himself in those fields only yesterday and many yesterdays.

She desperately wanted a day off for grandma: A blessed day without having to square the towheaded terror's devilment with her ultra civilized Tsarskoye Selo world of Palm Beach. She loved the imp but his antics were over the top. She gave her little darling some money for the movies, got hold of his due library books, got hold of the miscreant himself and marched him into the Dodge for a day in West Palm Beach.

And the troubled inhabitants of Clarke and Seabreeze Avenues breathed a sigh of relief and blessed her name as she and Joey delinquent had disappeared.

The old girl was a doting grand-parent but now she needed a day without him before she went into shell shock.

Her own Little Caesar and his juvenile delinquent pirate crew had been raising destructive hell in the neighborhood. This was terribly embarrassing and difficult to explain away down at the bath and tennis club during an otherwise calming afternoon at the bridge table, even after several sloe gin cocktails.

Duly dumped on Clematis, little Joey returned the due books at the old Memorial Library.

He took to the streets to discover whether either of the local movie houses which catered to the parent generation's burning desire to get the kids out of the house "before-they-drive-me-nuts" which supported a baby booming Saturday matinee market were showing anything new.

They were not. He'd seen it all last Saturday.

Undaunted by that temporary setback, the apple of grandma's eye looked for amusement among the oldsters congregated in shaded areas with card tables the city provided back then.

The old boys were busily engaged in the practice of cheating one another at games of poker and rummy.

It was also there where the old folks amused themselves on the shuffleboard courts (where the children's fountain is located in the West Palm Beach of today's world). Neither of these diversions are there now but at the time they were popular with seniors.

The heat was cranking up to a sunstroke level already and our boy retreated into the library for the needful solace of air conditioning.

Joey dashed past the band shell (which is now but another forgotten relic of a bygone West Palm) and into the library.

He entered and busied himself in the perusal of its tall to him bookshelves.

He carried various items that could spark his fantastic infantile imagination to one of the tables for closer perusal. He looked at all of the colorful pictures in those mighty volumes with the interest (if not the grasp) of a real, live scholar.

"Study" got old after a while so he put the books away and returned to peer at the big stained glass window which was at once the centerpiece and the namesake of the Memorial Library: That erection had been built in memory of the fallen servicemen of World War I.

The murderous sun outside filtered gently through the stained glass colorfully. It magically illuminated the touching scene (The home folks went in for those during and after World War I.). In it a dying doughboy lay dying in his trench. He sees a gloriously beautiful angel winging earthward to bring him to his eternal reward for sacrificing himself so gallantly in that war to end all wars.

That moving representation inspired in the little brat a selfless desire to wing to glory for whatever just cause war profiteers were selling that day.

But his ardent desire was all mixed up with the fear and awe attendant on such a fearful challenge.

It had been a challenge taken up in the recent past by fathers and grandfathers and great, great grandfathers in a long, long trail of wars that just had to be fought promptly every twenty years by the latest crop of "doughboys" stamped out of the national mold.

Boys were born to fight the next one ever since this boy could remember, and over many long years and centuries before anyone he ever knew could recall.

From time immemorial the citizens of this earth and this country have been perennially wrapped up and devoured in a deadly flytrap of never ending War.

Here at home that state of affairs has led to a nervous existence in all of our families lives: For the males were eternally marching away to and (some-times) returning from endless cyclic local and global dustups with robotic regularity. At the same time the females of those families concerned were continually and dutifully marrying, birthing and saying goodbye and hello to their sons and sweethearts at the convenience of the government.

Everyone that the young boy could ever have remembered knowing in that bygone day, and all of those he would ever meet in his future, had adapted to that furiously upset state of conflict and return (in or out of a body bag).

An ever present threat of war and eternal uncertainty as to what tomorrow might bring was presented to their credulous eyes by warmongering propagandists. All were sorely afflicted by the demands that the world of war had put upon them and yearned for a free, unfettered existence. Assuming such a thing might ever be imagined.

Had there ever been such a miracle?

No one could remember it.

But Joey was a boy now and such ideas never occurred to the eight-year-old mind. All he knew was he was tired of hanging around the library and soaking up its serious old atmosphere and air conditioning for now.

Running past the clock he saw that "gra' ma" wouldn't be back to pick him up for another hour or two. He had to find another diversion now.

A waiting cohort of hungry pigeons, perched on the second story of the Palms Movie Theatre. They watched and waited for anyone to drop food high above the shuffleboard courts.

The devil in Joey brought him inspiration: The jovial imp entered the Palms, not for movies he'd already seen, but solely for the purpose of buying two bags of popcorn with a motive in mind.

Now the scene was set.

The tyke strolled toward the shuffleboard courts creating the illusion of childlike innocence.

The pigeons watched ravenously. They were tense and ready for their big moment in the coming drama.

They sensed excitement in the air.

The shufflers shuffled on, innocent of any inkling of the awful fate in store for them.

Then a volley of popcorn was cast upon the courts of action!

Then another!

The pigeons flew down fast to eat the corn and disrupt the games.

The players, still unaware of the boy's plot, cried out in alarm: "Take 'em th' other way, kid!!! . . . . GET 'EM OFF DA COURTS AWREADY!!!"

The kid ran for his life before the old folks could figure out that they and the birds were only pawns in his cockamamie chess game.

So much for that particular brand of merriment. Grandmamma 's little angel had to cast about for a new kind of fun.

He hoofed it over to a car dealership across from the town entertainment center.

There was a big crowd gathered there, a lot of excitement and best of all it was also air conditioned.

And what was the red hot news sales pitch being huckstered over there?

"Hitler's Armored Limousine!!!

"Coming to you courtesy of World War II (you know—the war that had followed directly after the war to end all wars).

"The war's over, ladies and gents, and this is part of the spoils of war: The great dictator's own personal armored car!"

The salesman in charge of this public presentation was quick to point out the several points of interest.

Two department store dummies were seated in the ill fated conveyance: The stiff in the driver's seat had a trench coat and boxy German helmet with S. S. lightning bolts inscribed on the side. The dummy in the back seat, which also wore a swastika on its trench coat, a Charley Chaplin moustache and a high topped German officer's garrison cap obviously represented Hitler, the little sorehead himself.

The drummer went on and on about the impenetrable invincibility of this glorified war wagon, and the kid's curiosity was piqued: "WASN'T HE IN TH' MIDDLE O' GERMANY SURROUNDED BY HIS OWN GUYS, SIR?"

"That he was, my young friend."

"THEN . . . WHY WAS HE AFRAID?"

"That's a darn good question, son . . ."

But the darn good question went unanswered that day.

Soc Trang, Mekong Delta, South Vietnam (when there was one), 1962:

It is later on in our boy's life.

Now he is not in South Florida.

He is in another tropical mosquito swamp: America's then vacationland, Vietnam.

He's a young marine now, and he and his comrades in arms are up past their necks in an undeclared war on the other side of hell.

H. M. M. 362, his helicopter squadron had been sent there post haste when the Army Helicopter Company holding a Vietnamese bishop/rice broker's turf and keeping the Viet Cong from slitting the greedy little capitalist curate's gullet was mortar barraged into Nirvana by the V. C.

The Army unit had taken an eighty percent loss of both lives and accoutrements (including their chopper birds).

They were unable to continue the mission, there being eighty percent dead, and the marines were sent in fast.

The war the Pentagon would not admit was going on in Nam had used those poor souls both savagely and, in most cases, fatally.

The helicopter company was wiped out.

But after the marines had secured the area and taken over the old Japanese W. W. II airfield at Soc Trang there were no follow up mortar barrages against us.

"What th' fuck? Over—" we all asked.

Our marine unit was engaged in a couple of "staging areas." That is what a shifty eyed Pentagon calls a battle that it does not want to call a battle in a war that it doesn't want to call a war.

But Joe's squadron and its members were as lucky as troops in that or any war are:

The marine squadron only lost one bird. Unfortunately all seven hands aboard her were fatal casualties.

She was aloft on a test hop. And some V. C. dink of a sniper on the ground got off a lucky shot and hit the aircraft. It was a strange happenchance because usually the gooks weren't able to hit the side of a barn.

Her skipper panicked and was unable to successfully auto rotate her down for a soft landing.

As everyone in the Marine Air Wing knows, "It's not those long falls that kill you. It's those short stops."

The rest of our boys were able to return stateside for another try at getting killed on our nation's bustling freeways.

Those who actually made it to old age were even able to collect their war benefits in 1998 when a tardily grateful Congress at long last was forced by the facts to admit that there was actually a war going on in Vietnam prior to1964. But for the thirty-five long years in between 1962 and 1998, the pre-Tonkin Gulf combat veterans of that wretched war went unrecognized.

The 362 marines got a Vietnamese presidential unit citation from the greasy little dictator of South Vietnam and a Vietnam Expeditionary Medal from Washington. But we got no credit for being combat veterans of that shoddily hidden war for over a quarter of a century. The secretary-butted paper shufflers at the Pentagon who never spent a split second in combat with enemy ammunition coming at them saw to that.

The big buzz in tent city, Soc Trang, when Joe was there was that there was going to be a general inspection of their base in the middle of a red hot combat zone.

Well, that made as much sense as anything did in the strange world of a Mekong Delta combat zone.

So Joe and the others bitched like lifers and did their best to spit shine the mud. All of them were angry at the stupidity of having to put up with an I. G. in the middle of a war.

The troops didn't like it but they did their best to square away their quarters. They cleaned up offices, shops, mess tents and storage areas and Gunked down their birds on the mat.

The big day arrived at long last:

At first there was a distant silver speck somewhere high above them in a far off region in the stratosphere.

Shortly that speck began its long descent to the landing field.

As the speck circled for a landing it became evident that it was one of those huge air service troop and cargo carriers headed for our humble little ex-Nip airdrome.

We enlisted men were standing by our tents, the officers and senior noncoms were lined up by theirs and the birds gleamed in a neat row on the mat.

We were ready for them.—those chicken-shit bastards!

Now the flying behemoth taxied down the field, turned and came to a halt a little distance from the officers' tents. In a few minutes the big plane's cargo bay hatches opened down slowly.

In another couple of minutes the ramp was engaged and slid down to create a pathway for the wrathful entrance of the terrible inspector general.

Then a little armored tinker toy of a circus clown's armored car sped down the ramp, circled the flight line once and dashed nervously back into its big mama's womb.

The ramp was speedily retracted, the cargo hatches slammed shut, the big mama transport taxied without delay and made her rapid ascent into the endless blue.

"What th' hell was all that?" the marines wondered.

Top soldier Lucky came down from the mountain where dwelt the great god, Lt. Col. Zeus, and told Lance Corporal Joe and his buds what had just happened.

"Marines, that little toy car was occupied by no less a chicken than Secretary of Defense Robert S. McNamara, a skin savin' son of a sea cook if I ever DIDN'T see one!

"The good news is that since the bigwig was so yellow he never set foot outside his armored tinker toy he never found any discrepancies AND WE ACED TH' EVER LOVIN' INSPECTION!

"Th' colonel says, 'WELL DONE, MARINES!' And that goes double from me!!!"

A big whoop from his young troopers and stompers went up. Everybody sends up a cheer when his unit aces an inspection. because in the crotch it so rarely happens

But when all the shouting was over, one of the youngsters started to think:

"I've seen this movie before and it ended badly.

"When these so called 'great men' start hiding out in armored cars, that's nature's way of telling you something's wrong."

"LOVE, MOM AND DAD."

I was the kid in the last story.

Here is another one:

Tall, skinny Stembo Limbo, was one of our officers' mess stewards. And he sat facing me across a metal mess table aboard the aircraft carrier U. S. S. Princeton, which was under orders to take us to a point well within fly-in distance of Vietnam.

Until now we had been based at M. C. A. F., Subic Bay, where we had been chasing the HUKS, a Filipino version of the Viet Cong. As red as the Cong and as lethally elusive were the shifty, resourceful HUKS.

For the present we were assigned to duty aboard the carrier in readiness for swift transport when the word came down to go.

Dusky young Stembo's head was bowed and care lined his face.

It wasn't like the toothy, smiling Stem to be down. Actually, he was usually trying to spread some of his cheer to those gentlemen by act of Congress whom he served at mess (Of course, he couldn't do the impossible and the elect remained as dour as ever.).

"What is it, Stembo?" wondered I, "garbage can Navy food got y' down, kid?"

"White meat, I aint you kid, an' not nobody's BOY," he replied petulantly, "So don' be playin' no mind games wif me!"

"Oh," needled I, "you is gittin' ready t' boin down mah ole plantation house . . . That's how it is?"

"Naw . . . It's not lak dat," the sun burst through his cloudy mood at the hint that he wasn't able to take a ribbing, "You aint bad, Joe-Joe . . . You 'bout da friendliest cracker here . . ."

But the black cloud still hovered over poor Stem.

"Dish it up then, mammy-jammer," said I.

"OK . . . 'Member las' month when I pulled liberty in Olongopo 'n' come back wif a dose o' clap?"

"I didn't know about it."

"Well, daps jus'how it were, bro," he confided, "They decide t' fly me ovah t' Cubi Point Navy Hospital t' git it cured . . ."

"So? . . . What's th' deal? . . . Couldn't they get rid of it?"

"Oh, yeah . . . That were no prob.' It was what hapent on da way up t' Cubi!"

"Dish."

"What pass wif ME dat day should never ought 'o be tolt . . . but . . . but . . . it weigh so heavy on me . . . I jus' GOTS t' tell it t' SOMEONE!

"This bes it:"

On the Subic Bay runway early in the morning the little congregation of sick marines were lined up beside the chopper for Cubi waiting for the pilots to kick the struts and get them aloft. They were Stem, a couple of junior noncoms, the crew chief and his first mech, two pilots and a mysterious Navy corpsman carrying a big black bag.

The whole gang boarded the bird and winged skyward bound for Cubi Point.

The sole reason why Stembo did not need to be heavily sedated for this hop was that he had not been told this:

Yesterday one of the jet jockeys aboard the Naval Air Station there had been guilty of pilot error and creamed into one of the unforgiving cliffs above Cubi.

The crash fire had just about burned itself out by now and the corpsman, armed with a body bag, was on his way to pick what was left of that pilot out of the smoking wreckage for return and burial. That was on the way to the hospital, so it was the first order of the day's business.

All good children, and Stem was one of these, from the town of Wayback, GA (located way, way back in the Okeefenokee Swamp) knew that the damned spirits of the restless dead can and do leap into and devil—possess the immortal soul of the hapless living creature. The children of The Reverend Nate's swampy Sunday school class, including Stem, all knew that to be "Bible truth."

The chopper crew told their guests en route of the mission of the corpsman with his big body bag.

Stem had seen enough ornery white boy pilots to know that they must be Satan's spawn!

Now, as the reality of what was to be sunk into his brain, he began to sweat bullets and pray for some miraculous deliverance from what he knew must be the awful fate that awaited him.

Stem was a marine like the rest and able to deal with real danger; but this supernatural peril had unmanned him.

He could not let them see it. For no one else in the squadron had the advantage of being schooled in the swamp. They could never understand the eternal doom that was now hanging over all of them.

The gang landed at the fatal crash scene.

The crew chief and the corpsman searched the still smoking wreckage and quickly returned with the body bag.

By whose feet did the corpsman set that awful instrument of damnation?

You guessed it—Stembo Limbo.

"NO!!!" screamed Stem's tortured Psyche from deep within his brain as he anticipated writhing in hellfire forever.

His heart thundered right through his sweat—soaked shirt.

The aircraft climbed aloft into the endless blue.

Stem, still trying to play it cool, tried gingerly (in the vain hope of avoiding the attention of the others) to distance himself from the object of certain doom.

At about a thousand feet the pilot banked so sharply that part of the dead man's arm, a charred hunk of flesh, rolled out of the bag and came to rest directly between the terrified Stem's feet.

There was an intact patch of skin with the tattooed image of a valentine like heart in which the motto "love, mom and dad" was inscribed.

Stem thought he was going directly to hell nonstop and immediately lost his mind: He had to escape this unholy place and he tried with all his might to hurl himself out of the cargo hatch and into the empty sky below to certain death.

His shipmates restrained him and strapped him fast to a seat for the remainder of the flight.

Stem stayed at the hospital until his pox was cured.

(And a little longer for psychiatric evaluation.)

The Navy shrinks on Cubi opined that he was just a superstitious booby and recommended that he have a consult with his own squadron chaplain.

"What 'd th' sky pop say, Stem?" I questioned him.

"Dat jive cracker say dem swamp ways bes jus' a bunch o' backwards superstitions," he grumbled indignantly, "Den he read some parts out de Bible t' back up what he said."

"What d' YOU say?"

"He white anyway!.. Crazy, too . . . I never did understan' a word dat jive honky say."

"Oh, well . . . Let's go hit th' liberty launch t' Olongopo 'n' see can we get y' dosed up again so you can do you're thing all over again."

"Now I KNOW you alright, Little Joe!

"You makes a whole world more sense dan dat mealy mouf ole sky pop do!"

THE FLYING FISH

If you have never been a marine who is exiting the Philippines where you had been chasing HUKS to go to Vietnam to pursue the V. C. aboard an aircraft carrier so much the better for you.

But my comrades and I were just that.

Aboard the carrier activities were calisthenics on the flight deck, boxing bouts in the smokers, gymnastic exercises to get you ready for the boxing matches but no more practice hops. Our pilots and we of their air and ground crews were all practiced up for the hop because we'd seen it rock in the Pentagon's other "top secret" Filipino HUK War.

The commissioned worry wart powers that be think of everything to take your mind off of your likely lethal situation except for actual relaxation. A practice known to them as "goofing off."

No. Goofing off is left to the personal initiative of the individual marine.

When it came to goofing off this marine was just dripping with personal initiative.

There was the eternal card game in the crew-space where you, as a junior man, could and invariably did lose all of your money in the first couple of hands of poker, rummy or spades.

Then there were the hiding places where you and your pals could go sub rosa just to relax and gab.

The forward gun tub was just such a welcome avenue of escape.

There my buddy, Cousin Roy of Lookatabigfish in The Great Smoky Mountains of Tennessee and I were lazing high above the bright blue and white foam of the ship's wake on a picture perfect day above the waves of the South China Seas.

The entrancing beauty evidenced within the endless ebb and flow of the ocean's currents below and the overhead dome of sunlit sky above mellowed us out considerably.

Where we were and what we were up to were all but forgotten for now. War and destruction had been pushed aside to reveal an awe inspiring panorama before our becalmed eyes. And, for the moment, we were living the life. For in this time frame we were rocked in the cradle of that eternal motion of Creation in action which surrounds us unnoted for the most part in the glory of each passing day.

Incredibly, all of this boundless magnificence was only a pretty backdrop for that particular day's heart-stopping main event:

Suddenly—without fanfare nor a hint of warning to alert us—the star of the big show made her entrance in luminescent splendor:

Brilliantly sky bound and in a kaleidoscopic multicolor sea-to-sky ballet, a school of flying fish arched high ahead before the carrier's prow and winged, a mythic wonderment before our wide-eyed stare.

Their gossamer, pulsating fins propelled them on high before us and agitated the sun-drenched foam to create a brief and beautiful rainbow of light show opulence. Then they dove back deep down into Poseidon's realm.

We had no words to make anything resembling an adequate comment to do justice to that kind of transcendent natural beauty.

So we just stood there, as the old saw sayeth, with our faces hanging out.

It was then that the three hundred pound pride of Lookatabigfish shifted his giant feet in apparent nervous discomfort and spoke, "Wall, I'm in Dutch wif th' ole man, th' off' cer uv th' day 'n' them squirmin' m. p. snakes . . ."

And his mammoth jowls sagged dolorously.

"Whadja do now, Roy?"

"Whah . . . you know ME, Joe . . . I haint never done nothin' wrong in mah born days . . . . But them flea-bit swamp rats, Brer Bear Quantrel 'n' Snaggletooth Twit has now done got me in t' more hot water than ye kin shake yer dick at!

"And jus as soon 's we git offen this here chicken-shit Navy tub 'n' safe 'n' snug inter a Nam combat zone I gone blow bof them skunks inter th' nex' world 'n' say th' V. C. done it!"

"What happened with you boys that y' want 'o blow our two little shipmates from th' sticks out o' their socks? . . . I realize they're nothin' t' write home about, but—"

"THEM TWO AINT NO MORE SHIPMATES O' MINE THAN WUZ GOO-GOO EYES!!!" was Roy's furious reply.

"Goo-goo Eyes was a different story: He was the squadron sergeant major with a lot o'power he used for evil: He saw to it that I and a lot more of the junior men went to t' th' brig by stackin' th' cards against us and influencing th' colonel when we were over a barrel . . .

"I remember how he drooled 'n' gloated over me when the brig chaser came down t' run me down to th' lockup:

"'Now I got y,' Delta!' was his spiteful hiss.

"He deserved what we did t' him . . . AND MORE."

"That-there slimy swamp critter shore as hoodley-hey did!" grinned Cousin Roy.

The saga of Goo-goo Eyes:

First Sergeant B. A. Cannibal had been the author and prosecutor of every junior man's misery in Squadron 362 who had been unfortunate enough to be below the rank of E-5.

Ever since he had been appointed sergeant major of the newly formed squadron of young-boot camp-to—on-the-job-training-to-war marines had been suborned from everywhere in the Corps he had shown us an angry chip on his shoulder against our band of new boys.

His whole problem was that he knew he did not even belong in the crotch.

The fierce judgments and inordinately harsh punishments he regularly imposed on the junior men under his command were anything but unbiased.

His hatred of his juniors had stemmed from the fact that he knew that he was less a man than any one of us.

He was a human jellyfish without a single solid muscle in the whole of his stooped and sickly frame. Recruit Cannibal had enlisted in the Corps toward the close of W. W. II.

The drill instructors of the period thought this must be some kind of joke and were unanimously prepared to send little B. A. back to mama before he fell down and hurt himself.

But the officers of that day thought that a wimp like this little wash-out who had been gutsy enough to aspire to be one of the best was "cute."

Ergo, Cannibal was sick-passed through boot camp. Then the higher-ups trained their pet monkey to sit up and beg in the safety of the headquarters office from behind a typewriter.

That way the big kids couldn't get at him to peck him to death in the field.

This went on for years and decades as, sickly and underweight, the gentlemen's pet was excused from quarterly physical evaluations and outdoor field problems.

And he was regularly promoted.

This loathsome hothouse flower of a marine had been babied along and advanced in rank until he had become a first sergeant and.by the time he came to us as our sergeant major (a position of great power and personal influence on our commanding officer) his bile was at the boiling point.

Now he was ready to take his revenge against such hearties as he knew had always laughed up their sleeves at First Sergeant Pussy (and still did).

He had always hated and shrunk from the real men who had made the United States Marine Corps a worldwide feared and respected hallmark of military excellence, and he took it out on us.

But all of his sending men to the brig and saddling them with "shit details" for that long, long year we spent in California suffering our frequent punishments beneath his pitiless thrall backfired on the wretch when we were dispatched overseas to a shooting war: A place where the beast rules, and the hothouse flower dies.

A manifesto was posted one day on the squadron bulletin board when we were sailing toward Nam. It was penned by the junior noncoms and signed by every enlisted man in our unit.

It promised that the august Sergeant Major B. A. Cannibal would be our unit's first fatal casualty as soon as we got to Vietnam.

The colonel just laughed.

The men were fired with the fighting spirit to serve in combat so it wasn't mutiny. But they were just as determined to rid themselves of their number one enemy, the martinet, Cannibal.

Our colonel was a real marine who had already distinguished himself in action during the Korean War. He dismissed the proclamation as a stunt.

But Goo-goo begged him for a transfer out.and tipped his cowardly hand.

NOW the omnipotent Zeus knew how Goo-goo Eyes was and understood why we wanted to "blow off a little steam" by "standing up to him."

But the officers' favorite pampered poodle showed his yellow streak at once. He had never in all his years seen combat, let alone been surrounded by three hundred enemies he knew were conspiring to murder him as soon as they landed.

He begged the old man for a transfer. The colonel felt the same way about a yellowbelly as does any marine and the darling Goo-goo Eyes stood naked at long last!

Our illustrious commander granted the crybaby its transfer because a war is no place for crybabies.

BUT Cannibal was not going to pose as a responsible ranking marine non com after his present tour. (1ˢᵗ Sgt. Cannibal had been dreaming of a cushy retirement with lots of privileges and benefits.)

But that was not going to happen now because the colonel wrote large in his file: "NOT RECOMMENDED FOR REENLISTMENT."

The old man made a special note of his sergeant major's cowardice in the face of combat duty in that worthy's record with the recommendation that the gutless creep not be allowed to reenlist.

That was what I meant when I told Cousin Roy that Goo-goo Eyes deserved what we did to him for the pyramid of numbers is effective even in the Marine Corps.

And we had all united to bring the enemy down.

But back to the South China Seas and our forward gun tub: "Cannibal deserved to die," I reasoned with Roy, "He knew it as well as we did; but why d' y' want 'o put bullets through Brer Bear 'n' Snags?"

Roy looked ashamed.

"Y' don' know th' story already?"

"No."

"Wall, hyar's whut happent then: It wuz our las' night aboard M. C. A. F, Subic—so it wuz th' las' liberty we could pull in Olongopo—'n' Iz in town a-lookin' fir a nice, friendly li'l' Flip gal t' nail down to th' Star Bar whar ye kin find that kind o' stuff.

"BUT th' onliest trouble wif troop movements is that th' hookers knows about 'em weeks afore any o' us do!

"Them workin' gals to th' Star knowed it were our las' night 'n' theyz a-chargin' four 'r five times whut they usually do!

"'N' that weren't th' worst uv it: Th' DRINKS thar wuz sky-high, too!

"Who should Slither up into th' Star in th' midst o' all m' miseries a-playin' like theyz m' bestest friends but Brer Bear 'n' Snaggletooth?

"Them two slimy bedbugs come a-crawlin' up ter me ever s' sweetly 'n' Brer Bear say this-here place warrant worth spit no how. Said HE knowed a way better whorehouse/bar overtown whar th' thar wasn't no such a thing as high-hattin' nor high pricin' th' customers allowed—'n' there th' gals wuz all of 'em friendly 'n' none of 'em never give nobody th' air.

"We done grabbed a taxi 'n' got over thar in a few minutes.

"I done bought bof them two crawlin' snakes a drink acause I thought theyz m' friends at that time.

"This were a much more pretty place 'n th' Star, really uptown!

"Iz so happy right then.

"We drunk our drink 'n' then split up t' hunt our quail: One o' them cuties a-dancing' in th' floor show done caught m' eye right off . . . She shore wuz purty 'n' little, like them Flip gals air.

"After the show 's over she come down on th' dance floor 'n' we got acquainted while wez a-dancin.'

"Ye gits familiarly acquainted right fast in them places. Afore I knew it, we done agreed on a price 'n' climbed th' stairs ter her sweet little girly-girly room wif 'er Barby Dolls 'n' Teddy bears a-layin' all over 'er lace canopied bed.

"But when I done skint down her skivvies I found out this was no lady, this was a Benny boy!

"Hot damn! . . . Them two done brought ole Cousin Roy t' A Benny boy house!"

(A Benny boy is a Filipino transvestite many of whom earn their livings as prostitutes. Filipinos in general are a diminutive and small boned people and for that reason—combined with their female attire and makeup—these perverts are easily mistaken for women.)

"What happened when y' found a stiff bone 'stead of a hairy hole, Cousin Roy?" I laughed, "Is that your thing now?"

"Taint funny, ye gawdamn cheap-shot artist of a brig rat!

"Iz ready t' git th' hell out o' thar!

"But th' door wuz kicked in right then 'n' there and th' biggest, ugliest, dumbest 'n'hairiest marine m. p. sergeant in this world or any other yelled, 'AWRIGHT, ALL O' YOU COCK SUCKIN' SISSY MARYS, GIT YER PANSY ASSES DOWN T' TH' PADDY WAGON BELOW DECKS 'N' PRESS UP YER COURT MARTIAL TROPS!!!

"'OR YOU KIN MAKE A BREAK FIR IT 'N' MAKE MY DAY!'

"Wez all drunk enough 'n' dumb enough ter make a run fer it 'n' escape—

"But take it frum Cousin Roy, little Joey, that's a big mistake-!!!

"Them-thar out sized-hound dog m. p. s done had their fun a-whippin' our sorry asses!

"Then they threw us in a paddy wagon atop th' rest o' that night's brig bound catch 'n' lef' us t' feel right ashamed uv ourselves."

The shore patrol sorted out their catch of the day in the Olongopo jailhouse and notified their units of their prisoners' presence at that five star establishment.

Early, early, EARLY the next morning our three 362 ragamuffins were picked up by our understanding duty officer and his sympathetic old pal, the squadron legal officer for transport back to the carrier.

These fine feathered young Ivy League grads knew their job well and set about the task of cheering up their less fortunate shipmates at once:

The o. d. informed them that he was personally inclined to remove the attributes of their manhood.

Not to be outdone by a brother officer, the legal eagle was at great pains to rally their battered, bruised and hung over comrades and he quickly made sure that those laggards realized that he was going to advise our all powerful colonel to give them six, six and a kick (i. e., six month loss of pay, six months in a Navy prison with its attendant considerate and loving marine brig sentries and a bad conduct discharge).

Then the bad boys were escorted back to the base under guard and turned over to the duty n. c. o. in disgrace.

Goo-goo Eyes himself put in his swan song appearance to gloat over them and make sure that they were assigned to demeaning yard bird stoop labor in the blinding sun and draining heat of the Philippines for that long, long tropical day. That was one of the sergeant major's favorite punishments: He waited until he knew that his victims were sore and hung over and then worked them hard and relentlessly in the mean, hot sun.

Cannibal was still around then because the colonel was torturing him for his cowardice by keeping him around like a lame duck in a vengeful shooting gallery until the rest of us took wing for the war zone.

On the following day the bedraggled trio were paraded to Mount Olympus where Lt. Col. Zeus Alastor awaited them, three deadly lightning bolts clenched ominously in his feared and omnipotent grasp.

"WHAT IN THE NAME OF THE INDY FIVE HUNDRED WERE YOU THREE LITTLE MAIDS FROM REFORM SCHOOL DOING IN A BENNY BOY HOUSE?" thundered the wrathful king of the gods, "THE MARINE CORPS FROWNS ON FAGGOTS . . . AND WHAT THE CORPS FROWNS UPON I PUNISH!"

"But . . . but we didn' KNOW it wuz that kind o' place, SIR," bleated the three lost and trembling sheep in the shambles.

"YOUR NOTORIOUS IGNORANCE IS NOT AN ACCEPTABLE EXCUSE, YOU BOOBIES!!!" was the commander's loving reply,

"YOU CREATURES FROM THE BLACK LAGOON ARE AN EMBARRASSMENT TO YOUR FAMILIES, A DISGRACE TO THE MARINE CORPS AND UNACCEPTABLE VERMIN IN MY NICE, CLEAN OUTFIT—AND THAT'S THE ONE THAT'LL GET YOU KILLED!!!

"YOUR LEARNED LEGAL OFFICER HAS RECOMMENDED SIX, SIX AND A KICK AND I WOULD BE DAMN GLAD TO GET RID OF YOU THAT EASILY—BUT your crew chiefs have gone to bat for you (ONLY GOD KNOWS WHY!!!).

"So I will keep you around till you bollix up ONE MORE TIME—AND THAT WILL BE THE END FOR YOU!

"READ ME??!!!"

"YES, SIR!"

"NOW YOU GET YOUR UGLY MUGS OUT OF HERE SO I CAN THROW UP, HAVE MY OFFICE FUMIGATED AND TAKE EIGHT CONSECUTIVE SCALDING HOT SHOWERS TO WASH AWAY THE DISGUSTINGLY BITTER MEMORY THAT BENNY BOY BANGERS LIKE YOU EXIST IN MY NICE, CLEAN WORLD!!!"

"See there, Benny-boy Roy?" I cracked on the poor old victim of circumstance, "You're still th' oak leaf king's best girl!"

"WHAH YOU LOUSY CHEAP SHOT ARTIST!!!" howled an enraged wounded rhino, "I'LL KILL Y' FIR THAT!!!"

The Smoky Mountain Leviathan aimed his two ton fist at my head and let go with all of the fury that had been pressure-cooker steamed up in him after many and many a ribbing from the other boys in our lash up.

But—luckily for me—I was an accomplished boxer back then, and I adroitly side-stepped the killer punch to shout: "LOOK, ROY! . . . . THERE THEY GO AGAIN!"

And my block was saved as we went back under the charming hypnotic state induced by the flying fish as they winged up from the depths once again to fascinate us with yet another of their lightning fast ballets by courtesy of the ocean's fancy dancers. These shimmering beauties from the sea commanded our enraptured attention with their radiant showmanship.

And our flagging spirits were lifted up by it.

Their brief flight made us glad to be alive in spite of all of our troubles and the danger that attended our fragile, small existences.

I, who have since those days, partied with one of Hef's playmates and ridden Doctor Leary's fantastic psychedelic rollercoaster to inner space have never found a sight so wonderful nor yet so magic as to rival the multicolored dance of the flying fish of the South China Seas.

T. R.

Joe speaks:

I don't know what you might imagine a marine helicopter squadron, circa 1961-2, bound for the war in Vietnam might be.

In our case we were a mixed bag of nuts and bolts from all over the crotch.

We had been flung together in martial haste to accommodate the Pentagon's hunger for warm bodies to sacrifice to Ares in Asia.

And I was one of those nuts.

I was tested at Parris Island boot camp and, because my General Classification Test score was over a hundred and I was not colorblind, I got a three year hitch in the Air Wing.

I, and a handful of others from my recruit series, had skipped Infantry Training Regiment at Camp Gieger completely.

After boot camp and boot leave we were off to the Marine Aviation Detachment for aviation familiarization at the Memphis Naval Air Station.

The other boots on Parris Island envied and cursed us "lucky bastards" because we didn't have to roll around in the mud in full combat gear at Camp Gieger the way they would have to do.

They need not have been envious for we were not going to play war in dusty, rainy North Carolina. we were going to fight the real war in the tropic monsoons of Vietnam.

After a month or so at Memphis we were hustled off to El Toro and there we were ordered to report to L. T. A., Santa Ana, also in California for on the job training as helicopter mechanics and electricians (mainly mechanics because the electricians didn't fly so many missions and not so many of them had to be replaced due to sudden death).

California had been the marines' jumping off depot for war in the Pacific in World War II and it remained the embarkation point for the wars of our time.

I knew the guys from Parris Island and Memphis for we had all come out to the west coast together.

The Memphis brass had put me in charge of the detail going out there because I was a p. f. c. and the nineteen year old senior man.

We were all dumb kids and I was not sure if any of my boys was dumb enough to jump ship and run off when our train made its various stops. But I did think that it was highly likely.

So I took up everyone's i. d. cards and pocketed them even as I took care to remind my boys that anyone picked up without an i. d. was considered a deserter and would serve hard penitentiary time for it when detected.

Sure enough, one of my yard birds lit out for Mexico at the El Paso stop. But, without a marine i. d. card, it was his ass and not mine.

I called ahead to El Toro to the officer of the day that Private O' Dell had made his bird.

Our gang reported as ordered there at El Toro with all of my boys with that one exception; and we soon began our o. j. t. at L. T. A., Santa Ana after the El Toro runaround.

Everyone else in Squadron 362 had been suborned from all over the Corps: There were grunts who had qualified, shops-and-office boys, parachute loft guys and maybe a half-dozen retreads.

After a year of on the job training, we embarked for the Far East by jumbo jet over the Polar route. The Pentagon wanted its new warm bodies for its Asian shoot-em'-up fast.

We were ostensibly to be stationed on Okinawa, but we were only there briefly.

We were sent almost at once to the Philippines, and pronto.

First we conducted air-sea rescue operations in a typhoon there where we fished soggy sailing crews and passengers out of the drink to safety in the middle of the storm.

Then an unseen HUK enemy was believed to be shooting at the m. p. patrol jeeps down in San Jose Province and the U. S. came at them with two marine battalions and two helicopter squadrons (of which we were the best one) to hunt those slippery ghosts who strike silently from hiding and then disappear into a crowd of smiling Filipino faces with ease.

After what seemed an eternity of fruitless and frustrating Huk chasing, the colonel got us together to announce that an army chopper unit had been wiped out in Nam, and that we were finally off to cremate the V. C. who did it.

When you are a kid dying a glorious death for whatever trumped-up cause is for you and we all cheered our lungs out.

Then, of course, three or four chickens put in for and got compassionate transfers back home.

But who needs sob sisters crying in their pillows when there's a war to fight?

I was a disappointed that Rocky, my good old Cleveland Golden Gloves pal who had taught me how to box, was one of the first chickens who wanted to go—but that's the breaks of old Nav. Air. Better known as air-breaks.

On the carrier underway for Nam I got to thinking, "I wonder what makes a retread tick?"

(A retread is a marine who, for reasons unimaginable to me in those days, has served his tour, been released and, after being a civilian for months and sometimes even years, has suffered some kind of mental lapse and reenlisted—AGAIN!)

Do they never learn?

Up to now we had been a bit busy for twenty questions. But now we were on an aircraft carrier that seemed to be taking a million years to get us to war, and there was nothing for us to do but play cards, so the time seemed right to ask.

I was already acquainted with a young typewriter jockey who was a retread who worked in the squadron duty office because Rocky the bully was always playing tricks on him. The mischievous Rocky had been the half-lit wag who had christened our office poge pal, T. R..

(A "pogey" is is a South Carolinian French creole word used to describe a person as an underage coquette and it was adopted into Marine slang.)

Rocky dubbed our boy T. R. because he wore a moustache and Teddy Roosevelt glasses and the name had stuck because his real name was Richard Chap, and his more scathing detractors usually called him "Little Dickey."

Of course, he preferred T. R. to Little Dickey.

Poor old T. R. and poor old Joe had already lost all of their skimpy scratch early in the perpetual Navy card game that has been going on since before the beginning of time and will last past the end of eternity.

T. R. 's rack was right across from mine and I was curious about retreads.

"Poor little office pogue," I thought to myself viewing his short, potbellied person, "Why would anyone want to re-enlist?"

Then I hailed him aloud, "Hey, T. R., how in th' fuck 'd you ever end up in th' Marine Corps—TWICE?"

"You writin' a book, fat man? . . . Well, leave th' chapter about me OUT, Joey-boy!" retorted our flaccid office boy pal, trying to talk tough to a flight line marine and get away with it.

But that is not done.

I actually rose and sat up on the edge of my rack (a miracle which usually required an act of God, an act of Congress and a screaming senior non commissioned officer all at once) and growled, "I just thought y' might want 'o volunteer the skinny b' fore I have t' gut-punch it out of y' . . ."

His protruding paunch in peril, our temporarily heroic office pogue quickly rethought his tough guy act:

"OK, y' big, fat bully," he pouted, "You know I'm a retread, but what you don't know is that I HAD to come back in!"

"Why?"

He hung his head, "That's a long story—"

"Get started then, son."

T. R. 's tale of woe:

My first tour was mainly out west so when it ended I had no trouble getting back to my mom's old apartment in Oakland when it was all over.

And when it was over, I was glad!

But I couldn't find a job.

I looked and looked and never came up with nothin.'

Weeks, then months went by and I was still out o' work.

But my poor old mom was needy and she couldn't support both of us without some money comin' in from my direction.

After a while even my poor old mother refused to believe that I was really trying and kicked me out of her place.

Then life got really tough: I stayed at the hobo shelters as long as I could. But, in a while, they gave me th' bum's rush too.

I had t' live out in th' street now, and, buddy, that IS a tough way t'go.

There was still no work, especially for a rumpled up guy livin' out in th' rain with only gas stations 'n' bus depots to wash up in (and now even THEY are startin' to give me th' fish eye).

I was literally down 'n' dirty.

This is Oakland and I am stuck outside in that nonstop, cold northern California drizzle.

Now winter's startin' t' come in early (Just my luck!) 'n' I'm startin' t' get sick. I know when th' first snow blows in I'm a goner for sure.

I got no hope.

I slunk along those dreary city streets not knowing why I was still alive for what seemed like three times forever.

NOW I'M DESPERATE!

I go down to a pawn shop and invest th' last dough I got in a Saturday night special and a reload.

I remember a little mom and pop grocery store close to my old lady's place. I don't care about right 'r wrong 'r nothing like that goody-goody ol' stuff anymore now.

All that stuff goes on back in a nice clean world somewhere far, far away from me. If I ever was there I aint there now.

I aint allowed in there no more.

Now I' m only allowed t' die like a lousy bum in th' street.

Well, no thanks, hard times!

They won't let me be respectable no more so I'm going t' TAKE what I need: I'M going t' steal it from THEM and survive!

So I cased that little mom 'n' pop's store studying the best time to pull my heist:

It was busiest early on in th' day, at noon 'n' after five. But in the hours between midnight and maybe four 'r five in th' a. m. nothing's goin' on down there.

I made my play in the wee hours before dawn.

Big, fat ol' mom's the only living soul in there now and she's asleep behind the cash register.

That beautiful cash register!

That cash register was going to be my whole future and my ticket out of th' cold, windy streets!

But the bell on the door jingled when I tried t' sneak in and grab it and Mom woke with a jerk.

The old coot stretched and adjusted her glasses. And then she smiled because she recognized me.

OH, NO!

MOM RECOGNIZED ME!

It froze me in my tracks. She knew who I was! But there was no turning back now for poor old T. R.

"Vot might mom do from you, yonk boychick?" beamed the maternal tub of lard, "Hew tont look zo good, malchik—Maybe a little chicken soup you should need?"

"THIS IS IT, MOM!" I coughed covering her with my thirty-eight, "GIMME ALL YER DOUGH OR ELSE!"

"SILI NEBESNOYE," she screamed throwing up her arms in alarm.

Then she suddenly cradled her head in her hands and rocked back and forth in her chair crying like a baby.

"THIS I GET FROM YOU, YONK MAN? . . . I'D HECKSPECT IT FROM SOME OF DA LOWLIFER PRESTUTNIKS AROUNT HERE! . . .

"PUT FROM YOU? . . . NEKOGDA! . . . NEVER! . . .

"YOU? . . . YOU WAS ALVEYS SUCH NICE LITTLE CHENTLEMAN! . . .

"PUTT NOW YOU COME IN MIEN SHOP TO PREAK A POOR OLT VOOMAN'S HAWT, HEW RABOLNUI? . . . HEW OOBWEITSA!"

"LOOK, LADY, I AINT KIDDIN'!" I growl, "THIS GUN'S LOADED!"

"AAAAKHHH!!!" she grabbed her heart, "TSERTSA MENYA!!!

"SEE HOW YOU KILL MOM?

"MINE POOR OLT HAWT IS ATTACKINK ME!!! . . . BOYCHICK! . . .

"DON' LET POOR OL' MOM, VOT NEFFER DONE YOU NO HAWM, DIE FROM THIS!

"BOLYE . . . TAZHKA MINYA!!!

"POMOGI, MALCCIK!!! . . . HELP MOM!!!

"VITOUT HELP MOM DIES . . . ."

Was she faking or for real?

There was no time to think.

"PLEASE, MINE POY, GIF MOM GUN SO YOU CAN DIAL HEMERGENCY ROOM! . . . TAKE PHONE! . . . CALL HEMERGENCY BEFORE MOM DIES!!!

I was starved, scared and not thinking so I did it.

When I had th' phone and mom had the gun she underwent a miraculous transformation. And from that moment to this my life has never been the same.

"Hookay, hew little creepola hoodnik," she said with deathlike calm, aiming my very own artillery right between my eyes, "CALL POLICE!"

"Come on lady," I squirmed, "I was tryin' t' help y'! . . . How about just lettin' me go 'n' we'll call it quits?"

"Is no callink quits for you, mister rat-fink criminal," she was adamant, "I shoot you?—Tont push luck pecause Cops just vill gif mom a medal for killink hew!

"NOW CALL!"

I thought about playin' th' heart attack trick on her, but she already knew that one. So I called and she took the phone and told them where to come pick me up.

HEY!.. THIS ISN'T SUPPOSED T' BE FUNNY, JOE, YOU CREEP!

Oakland's finest came along soon and took mom's statement.

Then they handcuffed me and, being California cops, they beat me up good before they threw me in th' drunk tank on top of Oakland's shabbiest.

IT AINT FUNNY, JOE-JERK, SO STOP LAUGHIN' AT ME!

Well, th' fuzz finally dragged me out o' my drunk tank and into the courtroom and threw me to the judge.

The judge looked at th' report.

Hiz honor looked me over and gave me a choice between four years in th' state pen or four more years in th' crotch.

I picked this; and, believe me, that was one real big education for me in sticking up mom and pop grocery stores!

Oh well, maybe it is kind of funny.

TWO LITTLE GIRLS ON
HIGHWAY ONE

Hypoluxo, Florida, 1991:

In the later half of the twentieth century I worked installing and repairing field irrigation systems all over Palm Beach County.

In order to design and repair sprinkler systems a man is required to buy the necessary parts from various pump stores throughout the county.

The Broward Pump chain operated in Palm Beach County at that time and that was were I had my charge account. All of the Broward counter men were characters, but my favorite loon from amongst the flock was a comical old cracker who managed the Hypoluxo shop.

We were both Vietnam vets.

But he had been an army grunt while I was an air wing marine.

We were brothers in blood, but he was the jealous brother.

He was always full of wartime brag. That was doubtless because his daughter worked there with him. So to impress her more than anything else he would launch into a blood-and-guts SERGEANT SLAUGHTER tirade of heroic exploits he claimed to have performed in the war as he waded on to glory through a sea of muck and gore.

I took it all in with a dose of salts. But his little girl was young and foolish enough to eat it all up.

He always concluded his extravagant MAJOR HOOPLE cartoons with the brag, "AN' THEY AINT NO DIF' R' NCE ATWEEN TH' ORMY AN' TH' M' RINES!"

I never argued the point.

Why rub it in?

But his sweeping statement did sadden me for a reason that he could never have guessed.

Simply stated, Vietnam was a war fought for arrogance, hubris and profits for the already filthy rich.

All of this posturing went on in complete safety while at the same time in the Oriental swamps over there we real men were laying down our lives so that the 4-f sissies and phonies who were our politicians de jour might preen and pose belligerently as counterfeit heroes in front of our national television news cameras.

The act went on and on and the omnipotent carrions of our glorified Military-Industrial Complex (a white collar crime organization which has run our afflicted country uninterrupted ever since F. D. R. lost his grip due to protracted illnesses in mid WWII) could rake in mega billions in war profits.

With all that green in their greedy little fists the generals and corporate big wigs continued to bribe their high priced lackeys in D. C. to start the war show over again.

The war waltz plays on and on—for the fun and profit of these well heeled grifters—without end. And a new gang of foreigners in possession of desirable natural resources are demonized and targeted for enslavement every few years.

My old Hypoluxo buddy averred that there was no difference between the army and the marines; but I am sad to say that there is a vital difference.

Soc Trang, South Vietnam (when there was one), 1962:

This time we were the Pentagon's puppets out there on the front lines of their latest neo imperialist foray into bloodthirsty foolery for profit.

Joe Delta

Soc Trang is thousands of miles and at least ten centuries away from anything anyone living in the modern United States could ever imagine. Unless, of course, you've had the dubious advantage of having been there.

I'll try to put you in the picture:

You are standing up to your ankles (and this is in the DRY season) in a far flung expanse of swamp water that oozes up beneath a never ending sea of rice and marsh grasses.

Two ton mosquitoes are busily draining all your veins of blood, and an unrelenting tropic sun is scorching your hide. You are almost on your way to believing that you are back home deep in the Florida Everglades and the summer of your discontent.

Then a wrinkled little old papa-san perched high atop his gigantic water buffalo comes slouching by: "Chow oon!"

You're way off from being back home.

You are a marine transported back in time to an bygone age in land even then steeped in feudal serfdom.

Our Squadron HMM 362 had been detailed there to safeguard the life and fortunes of a Vietnamese Roman Catholic bishop/millionaire rice merchant from the well deserved vengeance of his local V. C. revolutionary neighbors and enemies.

The above Viet Cong are the slavish coolies of their cleric/taskmaster by day.

By night they are bent upon slitting this capitalistic notable's throat.

A feudal fief was distinctly out of place in the Twentieth Century and so was a medieval slaver/bishop.

It was all part of a colonial setup that the French had set into motion during the reign of Emperor Napoleon III not quite midway in the Nineteenth Century.

Now the French had finally taken the hint and left Cochin China after their colonial slaves in Vietnam, Cambodia and Laos had been openly rebelling against their "Empire of Annam" ever since they had declared its inception.

The Franks had gone home after losing the most recent war which had lasted for about twenty years prior to our ill—fated American intervention.

The chief difference between the French and American occupations was that the French installed a native "emperor" to act as their fiduciary there and the Americans appointed a "president" to act as theirs.

Both "national leaders" were selected from a native Francophile gentry who were tested, selected and Sorbonne educated to run the show there. They had been wooed into the Roman Church and taught to be good little Frenchies in Paris.

The rulers of Vietnam for over a century had been these French-Vietnamese. They were the pet poodles of official Paris. These folks were still minding the shop in our day in the august name of official Washington.

That was also the case in regard to the provincial governors and local tyrants like mayors and our little bishop:

They were all French Catholics in a predominantly Buddhist country. They were capitalist overlords in a homeland which cried out for communism and especially for independence from foreigners.

These Parisian sons of Vietnam were without a home for they were even less than twenty percent of the population in a place they had once called home.

It was their home no more.

After terrific losses and not a sign of victory their French masters had abandoned their local employees to certain extermination at the hands of the reds.

But in those bygone Cold War days a pitiful minority without even a prayer of popular support could always sucker good old Uncle Sammy into an already lost civil war. All the hard pressed notables had to say was that if the majority were allowed to exercise power it would be a "commie takeover."

That's what they did and here we were, propping up yet another Batista style dead horse regime.

The quasi French setup was still the same under our intervention. Nothing had changed since unlucky Pierre's exit including the peasants' anger and their implacable hatred of the "round eyes."

Our dear little old bishop and his mandarin ilk had remained so out of step with reality that they needed a marine helicopter squadron of bullies like me to insure that they would live long enough to see the sun come up tomorrow (with any kind of luck).

There were two reasons we were debarred from pulling liberty in the town of Soc Trang: The first was that the sleepy little burg was unsafe at any speed for non—communists because all of the common folk were as red as Grand—pappy Ho.

The unvarnished truth was that a new mayor had to be appointed weekly from a dwindling number of diehard Francophile natives.

The local V. C. had murdered the last mayor and all of the former mayors every week for hundreds of years like clockwork.

If marines had showed up in town there would have been an "incident." That would have instigated an "escalation."

And with their undeclared and unpopular imperial adventure in progress the Pentagon brass could just not afford any more of those.

(Imagine the number of ex-mayors who must have bit the dust since the days of Napoleon III all those years ago.)

The second reason was that the A. P. C. (fresh water truck) carrying a marine m. p. armed with a fifty caliber machine gun on top of it was fired upon by the unseen enemy with reliable regularity.

(They were probably celebrating their murder of the latest mayor.)

Our base c. o. was a little old full bird colonel who had been a prisoner of war of the Japanese in WWII. As a consequence of this he hated our little yellow brothers passionately.

Ergo, some of his written and posted standing orders seemed a bit crazy to the rank-and-file.

But all marines do realize that a written order is so serious that disobedience of that order means a certain court martial.

The order which was the looniest and least compassionate directed all cooks and mess men to refuse to give scraps to the coolie construction laborers who were aboard the base to expand it from a small WWII Japanese airfield to a larger air base.

Vietnamese society was ordered along the ancient lines of a mandarins-take-all-coolies-get-zip economy. The bishop and his Francophile cronies were the mandarins in this movie and they took all of the rice that was grown by the labor of their restive coolie farmers and sold it to the highest bidders—often in overseas markets. That had left those farmers whose labor had produced the rice to starve.

The local laborers were delighted to come to work for the rich Americans in order to eat; and they were bound to beg at the mess tents because they were hungry.

They were pathetic. But our little old full bird had also suffered the curse of a chronically empty stomach while in the hands of Nipponese captors in the big war so the poor little laborers stayed hungry.

And then there was another written order, posted high for all to see. This one was about Highway One: "All personnel aboard the base are strictly forbidden to go near Highway One."

Highway One?

What a grand name for a tiny one lane band of dust stretching from North Vietnam all the way down to the very tail-end of the Cochin Peninsula.

This order mandated that anything that happened down on Highway One was exclusively the business of our native Vietnamese perimeter guard company and none of our business.

None of us were to mess into their territory for any reason.

The way things were while we were there: The only native inhabitants of Soc Trang, town or province, we ever saw were the beholden bishop; a troop of Vietnamese engineers and the coolies who worked for them to bring the post up to muster; and a charming little base barber.

The bishop was a jolly old soul if you were there to keep his head on his shoulders and we were. The engineers spoke good English, had Nam grass and beer, played a decent chess game and were all around regular guys. The poor little coolies working for the engineers were a never-ending source of pain to the cooks and mess men.

But that little old native barber was the star of the show. For he put all stateside barbers to shame: He would give you a soothing massage, hot towels and a shave and haircut.

That relaxed your revved up nervous tensions like a dream. There is always a terrific amount of tension in the life of a marine on duty.

Here were some of our Viet war tensors:

Not only were we there to defend the indefensible lord-high-mandarin-bishop from his people but we also had to fly observation hops over a province where our chances of being shot down were just about fifty-fifty.

And then there were the "staging area" operations.

A staging area op is a battle the slippery Suzy Pentagon denizens do not want to call a battle in a war that they are calling an "advisory operation."

We were a vertical envelopment taxicab service commanded to fly the native anticommunist militia in to its movements against the V. C.

This anticommunist "militia" consisted of a dozen or so highly privileged and hot-to-trot young Francophile company-grade officers in command of perhaps a hundred untrained and army surplus equipped little boy draftees between the ages of ten and thirteen.

For the Vietnamese this war had been dragging on for a lot longer than twenty years. And all men of service age had been winnowed out by the constant bloodshed.

The situation would have been comical had it not presented such a lethally clear danger to the marines: These trooper tykes had been press ganged into service, taught close order-drill for a week or less and marched out to the rifle range to familiarization fire their rifles ONCE!

Then these docile peasant kids were sent directly into deadly combat.

In other words, they were woefully unprepared for what they were getting into—especially the flying lead.

We marines laughed about it because we were all young and young men always make light of their tension by thumbing their noses at almost certain death.

Then off the flight crews went on those "flying lead" hops:

We would pick up our kindergarten brigade and head for the "staging area."

At the staging area, a village which even our scant intelligence had found had been occupied by the Cong, the slippery enemy had always heard we were coming days or weeks ago and already left taking all of the healthy villagers whom they had just drafted into their revolutionary cadre.

These lucky kids were unceremoniously dragooned into the Viet Cong forces whether they wanted to be party members or no.

The enemy also carried off any livestock, food and materiel that they would be able to use for their cause.

The reds had left only a few of their wounded behind to scare the sick, the weak and the elderly still left in the village into getting between them and us.

Then their partisans opened fire on us from behind the townsfolk for propaganda purposes.

Naturally, we returned fire and the headlines read: "Heartless American imperialists slaughter the weak and helpless civilians of a defenseless South Vietnamese village!"

Meantime, the contra junior militia kids who were supposed to be fighting this battle did what any terrified child would do when hell pops all around them:

They threw their guns away and tried to climb back into the choppers which at present were being ventilated from hiding by flying lead and were therefore less safe than they were outside on the battlefield.

The marines threw them back out onto the field of play even as the enemy's bullets tore through the skins of our war birds with a dull "thump."

(With our rotors engaged you could not hear gunfire but only the distinct thump of the bullets' impact.)

The fear crazed little soldier/coolie kids ran around and around in a panic while their gung ho officers shot the terrified children down in cold blood for displaying cowardice in the face of the enemy.

After what seemed a million years longer than the time that it had really taken to clear our crew spaces what with hot lead flying past us and the likelihood of going home in a body bag mounting with the passage of every second we stayed on the ground we gained altitude and got out of there fast.

Sending farmers' boy chickens who had been conditioned all their lives through to take crap from their notable taskmasters and not to ever answer back to do battle against seasoned V. C. chicken hawks was nothing short of mass murder.

And it was a miracle that we never sustained any casualties in any of those comic opera dust-ups.

Our tin-tappers in the squadron metal shop surely had lots of job security patching up the bullet holes in our battered birds.

The punch line to this great big joke on all of us was that the anticommunist militia boys were always credited with the victory. That was because, sooner or later, those six sick and wounded Viet Cong defenders were either killed or captured by those half dozen hard charging Francophile militia officers.

(After those cold blooded little rats had shot most of their own contra kids, of course.)

No news of our approach that made the Cong retreat was ever heard in any of the Western pro-colonial "friendly" press because we were "not there."

To the larger World press we were the "Heartless imperialists . . .'"

With all of that in mind we really needed that thoughtful little old barber's massages and the friendly engineers' brew and Nam weed to relax after contemplating those free fire zone idiot's delight operations.

Aboard our M. C. A. F. in Soc Trang we were all marines with the exception of five fine young army men who ran the base com shack.

"STAY CLEAR OF HIGHWAY ONE!"

That was the base c. o. 's clear imperative written and posted for all to see.

But on one bright and sunny day just before the rainy season Highway One was experiencing rural South Vietnam's style of bumper to bumper traffic:

Early in the morning we had seen a little old papa san putt-putt southbound mounted on his motorized bicycle drawn vegetable cart.

That was it till mid afternoon.

Then, a little after two p. m., beneath the withering stare of the broiling tropical sun, two tiny Vietnamese maidens clad in that country's traditional dress approached the base giggling merrily along on their ten speeds abroad on what seemed to be a festive holiday for them.

The girls sped blithely past tent city and pulled up short right in front of the com shack.

Oh, dear!

Could this be bike trouble?

All five gallant young cock hounds jumped out of their com shack to succor these darling young damsels in distress.

The innocent-faced young V. C. cuties were so quick on the trigger that it was all over faster than I can tell it:

They whipped their WWII Japanese machine pistols out from under those long dresses of theirs and murdered all five enemies of their revolution.

Five army lads lay dead in the dust of that far away road in a strange land nevermore to see their loving folks or the shores of home.

Marines stood fast as per orders.

The red chicks mounted their bikes and ran for it.

But before they could get even ten feet from their victims' corpses they had joined them on the other side courtesy of the Vietnamese perimeter guards' fast action and keen marksmanship.

Within minutes the two CIA goons in their little shelter half suits assigned to Soc Trang were on the scene trying to chew out the perimeter guards for doing their job. The spooks were hopping mad because neither of the girls had been left alive for them to torture for information.

The marines intervened and told the CIA creeps to beat it.

Outclassed, outmanned and outgunned, the glorified sneaks retreated whining, "OK . . . But we're gonna tell your colonel on you!"

Off they went with their pointy tails between their legs upward to Olympus to tell Colonel Zeus on us.

They were passed and brushed aside by the o. d. and our two brave navy corpsmen carrying body bags and rushing madly toward the murder scene.

The o. d. reasoned that it was not a good idea for his boys' morale to stand around looking at dead bodies right on our base. They might start to think about who's next or, even worse, why?

Thinking is not good for the troops.

Marines don't think, they just do.

We went back to the daily routine of ersatz reality in a combat zone: The traditional steak and onions supper was served at the mess. That night's movie in the hanger was to be a Jimmy Stewart-Kim Novak effort. Our colonel and his x. o. were still laughing at the CIA nitwits who had had the immortal crust to stick their big noses into the Marine Corps business earlier while they tried unsuccessfully to write us a reprimand for calling their bluff.

Whenever Hypoluxo told his gory war stories and ended up with his no difference between the marines and the army editorial, I was sorely sorry that there was a difference.

Had there been none five boys might not have been gunned down, and they might have lived to see their stateside friends families and again.

T. R. FINDS TRUE LOVE AT AN OLONGOPO BAWDYHOUSE

Do you remember T. R. Chap?

He was the office boy/retread who tried to rob a mom-and-pop store and got slapped with four more years in the crotch for his efforts.

The first story about him tipped us off as to what a genius our boy was.

Here's another:

The fellows in our squadron were always running over to the local whorehouses when they pulled liberty; but I stayed away from them because the first adventure that I'd had in a whorehouse was daunting: In Okinawa a hooker had displayed the brass to ask me for my wedding ring.

I felt cheap enough being married to an attractive, nice hometown girl and being in one of those v. d. farms in the first place and I said no and that pushy little chipey had had the gall to get sporty about it.

But most of our guys were either un—married or so thick-skinned that they could fend off any feelings of guilt by recalling the dear old drill instructor's salty saw, "When you came back from an overseas tour don't worry about yer ol' lady 'cause you'll find her like y' left her, freshly fucked!"

T. R. didn't have to worry about any such nonsense as nuances for he was unmarried, poor and likely to stay that way. He was definitely hooker available.

He and Don Malchik followed our c. o. 's sage advice and they always went on tandem liberty in the notorious Filipino port town of Olongopo.

That was because an American sailor or marine on liberty who went there alone could end up with an "Olongopo haircut:" The back alley gangs that plagued that busy port town were prone to behead American servicemen with their trustily lethal bolo knives after which they would divide the victims belongings amongst them. The gang bangers would then leave the headless corpses floating in the harbor. That's what we called an Olongopo haircut.

It must have been the heady romance of feeling free in the far away Philippines or the allure of the giant tropical moon over the port. For it was there that our little buddy, T. R. found his one and only love, the charmingly assertive Josephina.

Josephina was a gorgeous little thug who was best known for her aggressive and enterprising personality—not to omit her kittenish pugnacity.

T. R. met Josephina and was felled easily and at once by Cupid's flying dart.

The young lovers got intimately acquainted for a week or two in her home brothel.

For poor old T. R. it was a voluptuous paradise and he and his lady love were feasting on the ambrosia and nectar of the gods.

"I love Josephina, Don," he confided in his co-romantic pal, L. Cpl. Don Malchik, "Y' think we ought 'o get married?"

Here we must pause for a moment to examine the down to earth common sense and capacity for cool reason of L. Cpl. D. F. Malchik: Don did not have either one of those qualities in his noble young head.

I loved Don like the brother in arms that he was as did all of the boys in our squadron. For Don was a natural "people person" and his openhearted goodness and sincerity attracted a host of good friends.

But Don didn't have the ability to think things through in the cold, un-flattering light of real life cause-and-effect.

An example of that truth was when he had suggested that we all go to the Para-marine jump school because the silver wings that we might earn there would look so cool on our dress greens.

"All we gotta do is to jump out o' planes 'n' parachute down five times and we get our wings, Joe!" he enthused.

"We're jungle bunnies running around in th' tropics, Malchick," I reminded him patiently, "When do we ever get a chance even t' wear our greens?"

"Are you scared t' jump out of a plane, Delta?" scoffed he.

"Talk sense, man!" I corrected him, "I joined th' marines t' get killed."

"But what if we jump out of airplanes five times and live t' get our wings?"

"Well, what?"

"Not only do I NOT get snuffed, but then the hard-ass turtle heads in charge o' th' paratroop unit over there will admire our fighting spirit so much that they will get us assigned to their unit:

"We will then run five miles at five o'clock each and every morning. And then they will p. t. our asses off for the rest of the day and for the rest of our Marine Corps lives.

"Now look, Donny-boy, we are now in th' Wing where th' livin' is comparatively easy for a marine.

"Do you really want t' be a grunt's idea of a grunt 'n' go through that kind o' Parris Island boot camp with liberty every day for th' rest of your tour?"

"It could be a big adventure, Joe—"

"We're going to war—that's enough adventure for me.

"D. F. Malchik!" I guffawed inspired by my cheap shot demon, "Now I know what th' D. F. stands for."

"Alright, wise guy" he frowned beginning to smell the prickly heckler winding up for a pitch, "WHAT do they stand for?"

"Dumb Fuckin' Malchik!"

The infuriated ninety-eight pound would-be paratrooper let me have it with all his might and main right on the nose.

It didn't even hurt.

"I'll let y' have that one 'cause you're m' pal, mister mosquito; but don't strike up verse two!

"Swing on me once more and the next time I'll turn on the ceiling fan and blow your skinny little ass out th' window—AND that ass might just not be recognized by your darlin' mamma!"

Don did have enough sense to cool off and change the subject when I told him to wise up.

"Y' really want 'o marry one of 'them, T. R.?" questioned the amazed Donald F.

"I LOVE HER!" wailed poor little T. R. out from under the overpowering throes of his grand passion.

"Well," everybody's pal came up with the desired goofy answer, "if you love her—sure you ought 'o marry her."

But the walls came tumbling down one night when the beloved Josephina had left the enraptured and ardent T. R. for a moment in the midst of one of the many nighttime trysts to arrange for a room in which to slake their all devouring passions.

In Josephina's absence another of the more adventurous working girls who peopled the same establishment made her move on T. R. while his inamorata was absent.

The Josephina of our little pal's dreams had suddenly returned to find her steady prey in the clutches of a brazen rival.

Hot words—which my two buddies did not understand—flew back and forth between the two girls.

The fiery Josephina ended the argument by knifing her rival.

Then the law had come into the foray on the run and arrested everybody who had not been smart enough to run for it.

Malchik had escaped the crime scene in one of his rare fits of good sense epiphany.

But the adoring T. R. (true to his lousy luck) had stood by his best girl in her—let's just say—difficult to explain situation.

For that lack of reason our boy and his slashing sweetie were both taken prisoner by a singularly unsympathetic Olongopo police force and summarily booked at the jailhouse downtown.

All of their misfortunes only proved to our incurably romantic.hero of the piece, L. Cpl. Richard Chap a. k. a. T. R., that he and his toothsome if loca intended were truly meant to be.

Quite early the next morning the o. d. stood a trembling T. R. before the judgment seat of the mighty Zeus with a fistful of devastating thunderbolts.

The poor enlisted soul (emboldened by the shaft of Eros in his heart) had the rind to ask the angry king of the gods for permission to wed Josie The Knife.

He told the terrible master of Olympus of his intent to wed Josephina and take her home to get her away from the bad influence of her Olongopo whorehouse home.

The master of our fate looked down on our favorite dupe with an unusual degree of compassion.

In truth, our commander knew the boy was a little light on the upstairs level; AND he needed T. R. the office drudge to work in the office instead of polishing the good ship, U. S. S. Princeton's brig.

"Chap," explained our squadron's own big noise, "this is a hooker from a port town we're talking about.

"YOU are extremely lucky, youngster. that she didn't knife you for the change in your pocket and toss you into the bay the way these local gangs do.

"Take her out of this environment?

"Do that and she will just stink up the next place you put her."

T. R.'s face turned red and his knuckles turned white.

"I WISH you wouldn't say that about the woman I love, SIR!" he fumed.

"PERMISSION TO MARRY DENIED!!!" roared Zeus loudly to remind this little man that he was only a little man.

"BOY, DO I HAVE T' DRAW YOU A PICTURE?"

"But, colonel—"

"YOU DO NOT 'BUT' A COLONEL IF Y' WANT T' STAY A LANCE CORPORAL, SONNY," glowered Zeus Alastor from his throne on high.

"I've WASTED enough of my valuable time on your foolishness for one day, MISTER VERY TEMPORARY LANCE CORPORAL!

"Now, young shaver, you can return to your duties RIGHT NOW or I'll gaze into my crystal ball and see a brig chaser and a seven-day lockup in your immediate future.

"PERMISSION DENIED MEANS PERTMISSION DENIED AROUND HERE, YOUNG MARINE!!!

"Now you get into your office and get your daydreaming ass to work.

"AND you'd better ask our sergeant major for extra work just to keep you from woolgathering your way into even more trouble till we head for Nam—Dig it, cat?"

You have to feel sorry for our poor little hero when he is forced to face the cruelty of the harrowing truth:

That his sweet, flowery love-dream was over.

But now military customs and courtesies pulled his puppet/slave's strings and made him say with a broken heart in his mouth, "Yes, sir, colonel."

He about faced and went back to work.

LUCKY US!

2nd Recruit Training Battalion, Marine Corps Recruit Training Depot, Parris Island, SC early in1960:

"MOVE OUT SMARTLY, RECRUITS . . . MAKE ME THREE ROWS O' CORN RIGHT HERE RIGHT NOW . . . AN' I DO MEAN TO-GAWDAMN-DAY!!! . . . NOT NEX' YAR . . . NOT TOMORRAH BUT NOWNOWNOW NOW!!!!

"PRIVATE FUCKIN' MOONY, YOU THINK I DON'T SEE YE EYE-BALLIN' TH' AREA?!

"GAWDAMN IT, I AWREADY TOLE YOU CLOWNS NOT T' THINK!!!

"WHUT IN THE HAIL WOULD YE THINK WITH?

"NOW RECRUIT MOONEY THINKS I' M FUNNY!!!

"MOONY, YOU MISERABLE LITTLE SHIT-COOLIE, YOU REPORT T' ME WHEN WE GET BACK 'N' WE'LL HAVE SOME CHUCKLES IN MY HOUSE . . . JUS' YOU 'N' ME!

"MEANWHILE, MISTER SMARTASS MOONEY, YOU KIN JUS' LIGHT OUT O' THIS FORMATION AND RUN AROUND THIS HERE GRINDER (I. e. parade field) TILL I TELLS Y' T' SE-CURE (stop)!

"DRESS UP THAT FORMATION AFORE I COME DOWN HARD ON Y,' YE UNDISCIPLINED HERD O' SCRUB COWS!!!

"YOU 'BOUT AS SQUARED AWAY AS A SOUP SANDWITCH, YE CRAWLIN' LOT O' SHIT MAG-GOTS!

"MOTIVATE TODAY, IDIOTS, OR Y' KIN BET I'LL SEE TO IT THAT YOU NEVER SEE TO-MORRAH!!! MOVEMOVEMOVEMOVEMOVE MOVE!!!"

So spake Acting Staff Sergeant Bones, our first senior drill instructor, on the island whom we (most secretly) referred to as "Fat Bones."

We had been blessed with two Sergeants Bones doing duty as the drill instructors in charge of our platoon:

The worst one was the big, fat Goliath in charge of this present formation.

The second Bones was his first junior d. i., Sergeant "Ape Shit" Bones, who was crazy and sadistic—,but funny.

A case in point:

Ape Shit Bones was a born comedian and loved to entertain himself and us, his captive audience by using his own loony approach to humor. It was that of a sadistic cartoon artist.

One late evening Ape Shit Bones was marching us to our posts to stand interior guard on our various duty stations around the second battalion area.

He halted our contingent at a phone booth where our first junior d. i. picked up the receiver and spoke into it loudly:

"Sorry, baby, I can't make it t' night—I'm th' sergeant of th' guard tonight—"

We had to crack up even though we knew such unmilitary conduct was strictly taboo.

"WHAT TH' FUCK ARE YOU MISERABLE CLOWNS LAUGHIN' AT?" Ape Shit roared at us in his brand of mock but convincingly terrifying fury, "IF YORE LAUGHIN' AT TH' DRILL INSTRUCTOR IN CHARGE OF YOU I WILL WHIP EVERY ASS HERE AND THEN COURT MARTIAL AND KILL TH' LOT OF Y' RIGHT HERE AND NOW!

"DO YOU MIS'ABLE CLOWNS UNDERSTAND THAT?"

What an act.

But at this particular uncomfortable moment on an island made up of uncomfortable moments, hours, days and nights I was beneath the baleful glare of the titanic and brutally dangerous Fat Bones, and that meant real serious trouble of the dramatic non comical genre.

"Thank God," thought I silently and very much to myself to avoid broken bones by courtesy of Fat Bones, "Our graduation's this week 'n' we're finally gonna get out o' this part o' hell!

"In the future—whatever happens—I'll be someplace where I won't have t' put up with Fat Bones any more at least."

I was smart to keep my mouth shut while I still had teeth in it because I knew Fat Bones was a Gargantua that was so mean and so sneaky that he could thump you right out on the parade field while the Observation Unit was watching him beat you to a pulp.

An adroit and sophisticated sadist was required to perform a hat trick of that magnitude.

The O. U. was formed and sent by Congress to Parris Island in order to watch out for the kind of excessive brutality for which Marine boot has often been so deservedly notorious.

The Ribbon Creek Incident sent the O. U. south:

One night a drunken drill instructor had ordered his swimming non-qualifiers into Ribbon Creek, a tiny stream out on the rifle range.

But that night the harmless little creek was swollen with flood waters from a devastating hurricane that had just blown through South Carolina.

The instructor was a strong swimmer and he managed to save most of his boys, but not all.

Two of his boys were drowned to death that terrible night:

There was the inevitable big stink in D. C. and the Observation Unit was born.

(Nowadays all hip drill instructors know that you should not drown your recruits—unless they really deserve it.)

Whenever we were on the rifle range our own d. i. s were sure to march us out to Ribbon Creek and assure us that we were next if we didn't watch it.

Back to Fat Bones:

One time, when the O. U. was right there on the second battalion drill field, the slippery A. S. S. Bones had commanded me to right shoulder arms.

Then he smashed my rifle into the right side of my face and skull HARD as he roared, "SQUARE AWAY THAT DAMN PIECE, PRIVATE DELTA!!!"

At the same time he whispered into my pain-racked ear, "If ye fall down I'll jest say it wuz frum th' heat."

I did not fall for that is not done on P. I. because it's a sign of weakness.

But I did learn to watch out for A. S. S. Bones.

Right now he was eyeing me with his mean little slit eyes; and I was sweating it out and wondering what he was going to do to me now.

"PRIVATE DELTA, YE WORTHLESS, LONG-FACED LITTLE YARDBIRD, GIT YORE IG-NANT TAIL THROUGH THAT BLAMED HATCHWAY—RAT NOW!!!"

I ran as fast as I was able to comply with his gentle admonition.

But not even too much was enough for fat boy.

His massive paw snatched me off my pins as I tried to run past him.

Then he tossed me through the door and into the 2nd Bat. photographer's studio.

There was not much in there. Only the twitching old drunk of a photographer, his camera and a department store dummy's torso wearing a Marine dress blue blouse and a dress white garrison cover.

"WHUT AIR YE A-WAITIN' FIR, DELTA . . . A RAINY DAY . . . OR MAYBE A WRITTEN INVITATION?" grunted A. S. S. Bones, enraged as usual, "GIT YORE DEAD ASS INTER THAT THAR BLOUSE 'N' COVER 'N' SET IN THAT CHAIR FIR YORE BOOT CAMP GRADIATION PITCHER AFORE WE ALL DIES O' OLD AGE!!!"

I jumped into that outfit instanter.

Bones grabbed me and threw me in the chair like a rag doll and bellowed, "SET THAR!"

Now my beloved drill instructor moved right up close in my face and belched fire, brimstone and lots of rank garlic breath into my nervous face:

"YOU BETTER HEAR THIS LOUD 'N' CLEAR, MISTER PRIVATE-SMARTY-PANTS-SKIP-SWAMP-LAGOON-AND-GO-DI-RECTLY-TO-THE-CANDYASS-AIR-WING:

THIS HERE IS YORE O-FFICIAL BOOT CAMP PHO-TO-GRAPH FOR GOVERNMENT RECORD AND YOU BETTER DAMN WELL NOT SMILE 'N' FUCK IT UP! . . . DIG?"

"YES, SIR!" I bellowed.

"IF YOU MOVE . . . IF YOU BLINK . . . AND ESPECIALLY IF YOU SMILE, IT'S GONER BE YOU AND ME, RECRUIT DELTA!!! . . . YOU AND ME!

"I'LL TEAR YE APART WIF MAH BAR HANDS . . . AN' THEN I GONE DRAG YE UP IN FRONT O' A GEN-RAL COURT MARSHAL FIR DIS-TROYIN' GOV-MENT PROPERTY . . . AND TH' DISOBEDIENCE OF A DI-RECT ORDER!!!

"YOU JUS' BETTER WAIT TILL YORE OUT O' TH' M-RINE CORPS FIR TEN—TENTY YEARS 'FORE YOU SMILE, LONGFACE, ACAUSE THEY AINT NOTHIN' T' SMILE ABOUT IN HERE!!!"

He was surely right about that in my present fix.

"He's all yours, pal." Bones said to his photographer crony with a sly wink which he did not think that I had seen.

Winks carried their own special message of impending doom from the bone crushing menace in this tense, fear burdened air of Parris Island.

"OK, boot," grinned the shaky old alky behind the camera lens, "sit still, look right here . . . and say: 'PUSSY!'"

"PUSSY, SIR!" I barked right straight out of a Buster Keaton dead-pan mug.

Even A. S. S. Bones couldn't fault me for my dedicated display of stoicism.

But I had spoiled their perverse joke by doing as I was told, and Fat Bones was livid:

"YOU ALLUS WUZ A CHICKEN-SHIT-MOTHER-FUCKIN-'COCK—SUCKIN-'SOMEBITCHIN'-SMARTASS, HUH, DELTA??!!!"

Fat Bones jerked me up out of the chair with his left fist and gut-punched me HARD with his right.

But I'd had three long, rugged months in boot camp to get toughened up to that kind of rough stuff. This was just more of the same and it had no real effect on me to fat boy's disappointment and fury.

"YOU MIS-ABLE CLOWN, DELTA!" howled he, "YOU'D FUCK UP A WET DREAM, WOULDN'T Y'??!!!

"NOW YOU GIT YORE FLEA BIT HAUNCHES OUT O' THEM DRESS BLUES (WHICH YOU DO NOT DESERVE T' WEAR NIETHER) 'N' FALL BACK IN TO FORMATION OUTSIDE NOWNOW NOW!!!

"SGT. LURCH, SEND ME IN MAH NEX' VICTIM!"

I gratefully beat it out of there to fall into ranks and disappear from my two ton tormentor's awful rage.

(Moony was sweating it out on his thousandth lap around the grinder, but he was also used to boot by now. There were no more surprises for us now.)

Now it was Private Pest's turn in the barrel with Fat Bones.

Poor old ungainly Private Pest was a clumsy soul who had made it through boot camp solely by tenacity and the grace of God—like the rest of us.

Pest ran past me to report as ordered, and fat boy was ready for him:

"O, LOOKEE WHUT I FOUND UNDER A ROCK!!!" stormed our first senior big bully in charge with glee, "WHY, IF IT AINT PRIVATE PEST!

"YOU BETTER MOVE YORE NO ACCOUNT HIDE IN HYAR, IDIOT!!!

"YORE MAMMY NAMED YOU RIGHT, PRIVATE PEST!

"YOU SHORE ARE GIST A ORNERY LITTLE PEST!

"I BEEN WANTIN' T' KILL YOU EVER SINCT I FUST LAID EYES ON YORE UGLY FACE, YOUNG LADY!

"MOVE OUT SMARTLY, PEST!!!

"WHUT'RE YE A-WAITIN' FIR?

"GRANNY WUZ SLOW, PRIVATE PEST, BUT SHE WAS DEAD . . . AND IF YOU DON'T MOTIVATE YORE A-GUNNA JOIN GRANNY RAT TODAY!!!"

Soc Trang, S. Vietnam, 1962:

All of the seasons in Vietnam are even worse than our Stateside August steam bath. That's true even in darkest Florida.

This one was a bad, humid day all right; but at least there were no "kindergarten offensive" hops on for today.

There were just a couple of observation hops sent aloft to "secure the area."

As one of my own bird's ground crew all that I had to do was grease and clean the rotor heads, fuel her up and taxi her off down the runway.

Then I would wait for her to come back much, much later.

Till then there was nothing to do but wait for her to taxi in.

But there was hope and help for all of us attached to our squadron's ground crews:

The young, over-privileged Vietnamese engineers who had been sent to refurbish and expand our base would get caught up with their layout and planning end of that big job. Then they would have to wait for their coolie crew to catch up by doing their end of the job, the actual labor.

These engineers were the smart kids from that ten-to-twenty percent ruling class whom I have already so lovingly introduced.

They were first class chess players, and they always had a load of beer and Nam weed to share with their ground crew pals.

They spoke French, Vietnamese and very good English and they were top grade conversationalists:

We learned from them the history and inevitable revolutionary shift to social democracy and regime change that was then and had been in progress for all of their young lives and longer.

"What're you kids gonna do when y' grow up?" I joked them one day.

"We got to get out o' here, baby!" one of the leaders made reply.

"Why?"

"Those V. C. don' like us 'cause th' French did like us and gave us education 'n' their Roman religion and power over our workers," was his nervous reply, "Now those workers hate us and follow Grandfather Ho.

"Ho hates all round eyes except Russians.

"Because we always help our brave occupiers, he hates US."

"You got no worries with us here," we reassured them.

They weren't convinced.

"You are here now, but soon we will have to run for our lives to th' Philippines or Japan or even to th' States if we're lucky."

"Aren't y' gonna stay and fight t' hang on to your own country?" we wondered.

"Ten percent against ninety?

"I do not like those odds!

"We have been doing just that for the past twenty years:

"First we help Frogs fight Viet Minh!

"Then we help Japs do the same!

"Frogs come back when Japs go and we help them again!

"Now you come along with your neo brand of imperialism and we help you!

"Same long war—Viet Minh changed their name to Viet Cong. That's been the only difference in over twenty years of non stop warfare.

"The V. C. still fight on against us no matter what we do and no matter which round eye comes from overseas to help. They will win so we have to find a new home or they will kill all of us off."

"But we're here!"

"That army helicopter company was also here.

"But they are not here now because the V. C. killed them all off."

"C. M. C. will just send in another boot squadron to replace us if and when we get greased.

"Plenty more where we came from, to paraphrase WW II 's General Mac Arthur."

"But it will not matter here in this war because your countrymen do not have the patience of the V. C."

"Now that you mention it, we've been wondering why they've never hit the base since they snuffed those poor ol' dogfaces," I questioned, "I don't see why they couldn't just do it all over again."

Our Vietnamese brothers burst into a raucous gale of laughter at that, "YOU ARE JUST LUCKY TO BE MARINES, BABIES!!!"

"Lucky? . . . How's that?"

"Not your army nor nobody else's scare Viet Cong . . . But you marines TERRIFY even those cold blooded butchers!"

"How come?"

"We know the answer to that one first hand:

"When we were all kids from around here we all played together. (Both us AND the poor kids that grew up to become the local V. C. brass.)

Our then Jap forces of occupation used to show films in the hanger. Just like you do now.

"All of us kids snuck in to watch a free show!

"They played a Nip news real before the main feature and here's how it went:

"Hirohito's picture came on the screen and the Japanese anthem blared while their airmen jumped to attention.

"Then the narrator bullshit us on Japan's destiny to rule all of Asia and someday the world.

"But his voice became grim and ominous when he said:

"'OUR HONORABLE IMPERIAL MINISTRY OF INFORMATION HAS DISCOVERED THAT THE U. S. YANKEE DOGS ARE POURING SAVAGE HORDES OF UNITED STATES MARINES INTO THEIR INEFFECTIVE LOSING STRUGGLE AGAINST OUR BRAVE AND VICTORIOUS CONQUERORS OF THE EAST!'

"Then images of Jimmy Cagney and Georgie Raft are flashed upon the screen.

"Those gangsters' Tommy guns flash and their rivals' speakeasies are firebombed as they rubbed out their competitors in the prohibition era bootleging business.

"'IT HAS COME TO OUR GOD/ EMPEROR'S AUGUST ATTENTION THAT THOSE BLOODTHIRSTY MONSTERS RECRUITED INTO THIS CORPS OF CUTTHROATS ARE SELECTED FROM ONLY THE WORST AND MOST NOTORIOUS OF ALL CHICAGO

GANGSTERS!' continues the sound track, 'BUT THE WORST OF THIS MOST ALARMING NEWS IS THAT THESE DEMONS ARE REQUIRED TO KILL THEIR OWN MOTHERS AS A PREREQUISITE TASK FOR ENTRY INTO THAT CORPS OF BLOODTHIRSTY ASSASSINS!!'"

We all cracked up.

When the laughter subsided the engineer managed to say, "Japs were plenty mean! . . . They were savage fighters who feared no foe.

"They murdered the French; they decimated the English; and they slaughtered many, many Viet Minh. So, if THEY were scared of you, the V. C. fear you enough to not want to stir you up."

We all had another big laugh at how your reputation can make your most implacable enemy back off.

Then I said, "But th' Nips had it all turned around bas-ackerds:

"FIRST we're sent to a quaint little resort called Parris Island where we are coddled and fondled by our darling little nursemaids known as drill instructors.

"While these gentle nurses are babying us along there those gentle souls teach us a whole new and exciting language.

"Next we are sent home on boot leave.

"At home we try out our new language over at the family dinner table and THAT is what kills our mothers!"

THE BRIGADIER?
HE'S GENERALLY IN THE BRIG.

When first I joined the marines I expected them to roll out the red carpet because I believed that I was destined to be a red hot and combat happy career man and consequently a handsome corpse.

But unfortunately the Marine Corps never did a anything I told them to do.

I went after my dream when I was done with Parris Island and Aviation Familiarization in the Marine Aviation Detachment at N. A. S., Memphis.

At that time I had landed in an on-the-job-training squadron in Santa Ana, CA. I was lucky enough to be in a unit which was soon to see red hot overseas action in the Far East.

I opened my bid for glory by getting a recommendation to attend officers' training school from my own commanding officer and two of the more friendly and democratic captains I knew in my squadron.

Without even studying, I aced the required two year college equivalency exam with flying colors.

After that I passed my vision and physical co-ordination tests handily.

It had begun to look like I was headed for Quantico and then Pensacola flight school.

But that was before I was directed to report to some poof of a navy psychiatrist; and when navy lieutenant Little Lord Poof discovered that I had joined the marines for the expressed purpose of dying a glorious death in action the Tepid Tessy ventured the professional coward's opinion that I was too loony to be a Marine Corps officer.

I erupted!

"Didn't Chesty Puller make his name as a marine officer leading a pack of brig rats on a suicide mission against th' Japs because everyone else in his unit was chicken to go?" I demanded hotly, "Volunteering for a suicide mission would make him just as crazy as you say I am!

"How about the Dern Expedition?" I warmed to my subject, "One company of marines braved the murderous North African desert after they had already completed the then highly perilous task of crossing the wide Atlantic Ocean to meet and defeat every Barbary pirate in the world!

"Does that sound sane to you?

"NO!—But that's why the original Mamaluke sword was awarded to the captain in command of that Marine company by the king of Egypt for wiping the Barbary pirates off the surface of the earth: For being such a nut that he persevered against the sea, the desert AND the cutthroats who had all Europe scared shitless of their wanton savagery for hundreds of years!

"Their captain was also crazy according to you?"

"That was then," was doctor pansy's smug and perfunctory riposte, "This is NOW, p. f. c., and NOW you are Not going to officers' training school and you will NOT be an officer because I say so and that's that."

Navy lieutenant chicken-of the sea had pulled rank and it was quite pleased with itself as it put on its makeup to sundown it at the o. club.

"If an every day Beetle Bailey yard bird is what they want that's exactly what they're going to get," I resolved.

I and my buddy, Rocky Bite the Cleveland Golden Gloves boxer, showed up for roll call in the mornings and then faded away into the P. X., to the barracks to nap, to the movies and anyplace else to goof off like the ghostly escape artists we had become.

M. p. s were always writing us and everyone else on base up for this or that petty infraction of the demanding and stringent rules there.

Their rancid little show had quickly become a real live drag!

Then we found out why and took swift and violent revenge:

These basest of the base military flat feet had started up a monthly lottery to ascertain which among their band could get the most write ups in one month. Whomever won that cheesy contest won a keg of beer.

The tough guys from among our squadrons aboard the base caught up with the not-so-lucky winners in town and gifted them with a bonus prize:

A pair of broken kneecaps just for old times sake.

But those were just Stateside high jinks for kicks.

The epitome of our butt busting fun came at a time when we were stationed at M. C. A. F,, Subic Bay in the Philippines.

We were waiting there for our orders to go to Nam.

That was also the place where one Little Charley Birk (a toadying choir-boy variety of marine) had just made lance corporal ahead of me and I was angry.

Rocky the pug and I were getting rum-drunk in the tropics (Never a good idea!) on the night before the regrettable incident.

Rocky was a died-in-the-wool hood who was proud of how well I was progressing as a boxer with him as my trainer. He was anxious for me to have a bout—and at the same time—to put the recently advanced good little boy toad eater in his place.

"Delts," rasped Rocky the Instigator, "y' ought o' plow that chicken-shit Little Charley under!

"I'd kick his ass and then piss on 'im if it wuz me."

"It roasts my acorns the way they give a dink like him rank for bein' his fuckin' crew chief's sweet little Nancy boy!" slurred I in my turn.

My own hurt pride, the tropics and the strong rum combined with Rocky's red hot rhetoric ganged up on me and drove me on and on to a state of insane fury.

With the seasoned good judgment of a pair of twenty year old drunks The Rock and I got as lit as we possibly could and then stumbled back to our home squad bay to collapse.

Rocky had the good sense to pass out for the night.

But I was far and away too fired up for bed and stalked into the barracks—more of a juggernaut than a man.

I went directly up to the newly promoted Lance Corporal Little Charley cringing in his rack and said roughly;

"Get yer fuck-boy, chicken-shit, kiss-ass butt out o' that rack, mister nice little lance pig! . . . I'm fixin' t' kick yer fat caboose dead t' China . . ."

"NO!

"I . . . I done seen you put that fancy dancer away in them boxin' smokers aboard th' carrier, Delta," whimpered the poor slob, "I aint about t' fight YOU so just leave me be!"

The poor soul was faint hearted and fearful of my proven boxing proficiency.

But I was a drunken madman and not to be denied my insane vengeance and to my shame I humiliated my hapless victim by urinating on him where he lay.

(When I tell other Marine Corps veterans that story they always laugh knowingly and say, "Yeah, Joe, you were a marine all right.")

But The Uniform Code of Military Justice is swift to swoop down to take its toll and the powers that be have no such sense of humor while on active duty as they might in retrospect:

And the upgraded yet degraded L. Cpl. Little Charley ran precipitously away to the squadron duty n. c. o. to report my dastardly deed.

The dirty duty put it in his report and promptly at dawn of day the following morning our sadistic hothouse flower of a marine sergeant major, the one and only Goo-goo Eyes Cannibal, stood menacingly over me as I tried to sleep it off.

The old first shirt leered at my hung over prostrate form with a ghoul's relish.

"Now I got y,' Delta!"

And this time he did have me because he knew that the colonel's wife was a heavy and uninhibited drinker who had frequently embarrassed the great man with her alcoholic excesses back in the states.

Cannibal was confident that for this reason Zeus Alastor hated drunks with a purple passion; and the king of Olympus was sure to punish me good and hard enough for her and for me both.

Lt. Col. Zeus of Olympus was holding non judicial summary court over a raft of drunken offenders (but none as brazenly offensive as I had been) the next day.

When it was my turn in the barrel the colonel roared fiercely at poor little me, "SO YOU GOT DRUNK AND HAD YOUR FUN BY PISSING ON A SHIPMATE, DID YOU?

"SEVEN DAYS BRIG ABOARD SHIP FOR YOU, MISTER RUM-DUMB LUSH DELTA!"

A fat and cheerful brig chaser was summoned to the scene of my downfall at once and howled quite understandingly, "GIT YER WORTHLESS ASS UP T' YER BAY 'N' GET YER TOWEL 'N' SHAVIN' SHIT TOGETHER, Y' FUCKIN' IDIOT!!!"

My charming companion encouraged me to hurry along to the ship's lock up with towering oaths and more than one sharp jab from his sturdy wooden club.

The brig of the good ship, Princeton was nothing short of beautiful!

That is because all of the paint had been purposefully removed from the bulkheads and barred cell hatches; and the exposed metal shines like the noonday sun due to the great care of its inmates. For the reason why those walls and bars shine so brightly is that the men imprisoned there shine them with Brasso. Whenever all other lowly and demeaning tasks those prisoners perform aboard ship every day have been exhausted they are turned to in order to polish the brig.

Some of the other enchanting brig customs?

When you are sentenced to brig time your prisoner's head is shaven bald, you wear a sailor's cap and floppy dungaree coveralls and the genial brig sentries try to make things as much like marine boot camp for the prisoners as they can.

For we marines it's a breeze because we've seen the movie before

But for the sailors marine boot camp is pluperfect hell.

Some quaint brig customs take a little getting used to for everyone.

One such acquired taste is being searched every time you leave or enter the brig: You are spread-eagled clumsily with your hands spread out wide on the bulkhead while your feet are spread out even wider on the deck after the fashion of a gay Republican senator on the make in an airport men's room. All for the pat down search.

Then, if the sentry searching you is in a foul mood (and they always were), he kicks your feet out from under you and you have a hard time to save your face by falling on your skinned up palms and elbows.

Doctor poof kept me from being a brigadier general.

Now I was "generally in the brig."

One punk seagoing bellhop of a brig sentry used to brag himself up to his poor old captive audience down there about how he and his cronies had handcuffed prisoners whom they did not like to the pipes that ran along the overhead and used their clubs to beat those poor bastards bloody.

I did not like that little braggart so I waited until we prisoners were sent up to try to clean up a head which was overflowing with overturned commode water and human fecal matter in the middle of a typhoon.

What luck!

Brag boy was the sentry posted to direct our efforts there and he was already looking a little green around the gills just from the rancorous odor and the dizzying difficulty of trying to get one's footing in the midst of a storm at sea.

I waited for the ship to lurch beneath the typhoon's fury.

All at once she was jarred violently by the waves of the angry sea.

At that golden moment I pretended to lose my balance and threw a body-block into the counterfeit bad boy with all my considerable force.

I sent the brag boy sprawling right into a big, steaming pile of fecal matter to mess up his pretty knife pressed trops.

Punk-boy didn't even say anything to me.

That trip into the turds had made him sick and taken all of that spunk that he was famous for faking out of him.

Little miss sea school was too busy barfing on his own spit shined shoes and crying over his ruined trops to play the Terrible Attila role anymore.

It was fun down there below if you were tough enough, but the navy deck-ape prisoners really caught it in the lowly quarters :

One or another of them was always being put on bread and water combined with solitary confinement as a punishment for minor infractions in regulations that the guards made up as they went along.

I am a fast study, and a sadist rather than a masochist so it was all over for me in that one seven day hard lesson.

"Welcome back, Delts," smiled our squadron's executive officer as he shook my hand after my release, "I hope we won't be having to do that again?"

"Thank you, sir," grinned I, chastened, "Don't worry about a repeat performance out o' me!"

"I did a dumb thing, but I've sure smartened up considerably in just a week."

A SQUADRON BEER BUST AND A TORTURE ISSUE

About midway in our tour at M. C. A. F., Soc Trang the little bishop whose big bucks rice interests we were posted there to protect was overcome by gratitude to the extent that he threw us a lavish party with all the beer the entire Fleet Marine Force could have held down. That was accompanied by a huge main course feast of barbecued water buffalo beef.

Water buffalo meat is a just a tasty and exotic delicacy to delight a Christian gourmet. But to a Buddhist it is anathema and a gross insult against his holy Brahman cow hurled in the face of the faithful by those unwelcome foreign intruders.

Different cultures have different notions of propriety.

Ostensibly, South Vietnam was ruled by her fat little henpecked president, Ngo Dinh Diem. But the actual tyrant firmly ensconced in the Ngo family driver's seat was his horrid little wife, The Dragon Lady, Madame Ngo.

Now the comedy team of Ngo and Ngo were both devout Roman Catholics.

Fat little short round Ngo never rocked the boat in any way.

But his guts-and-glory gun moll was a chip-on-the-shoulder variety of Papist—a la Torquemada.

One pope or another back in the early sixties had voiced an aversion to bikini beachwear and our new dance called the twist.

Mme. Ngo had picked right up on this news and outlawed both the bikini and the twist!

It was such an outlandishly autocratic whim that not even Generalissimo Franco was dumb enough to follow suit.

That was how the South Vietnam of 1962 was governed, by the caprice of an unhinged Dragon Lady martinet.

She said, "Jump!"

And hubby said, "Yes, dear."

And if you were a young Vietnamese girl wishing to show off your good figure and dared to wear a bikini to a public beach you would soon find yourself in a tiger cage; or very uncomfortably seated and suffering in one of The Dragon Lady's private torture chamber in the presidential palace.

Similarly, if you owned a bistro that featured twist music you would find your choice of music both painful and possibly ultimately fatal.

Such was the "freedom" which it was our oh so happy duty to defend in the South Vietnam of that dark and dreary dictatorship of the goofy. The freedom of that implacably evil queen to torture her subjects.

Mme. Ngo was a madwoman determined to drive her realm further and further into the frenzied hell of her own rotten and unhinged personality.

That basket case in the presidential palace imposed savage and unbearable whimsy upon the poor people of her unhappy land, rebels and Francophile loyalists alike.

The beer bust was a festive affair and everyone got royally drunk. Some of us even got imperially sloshed.

Having heard of The Dragon Lady's latest hilarious ukase, one of our good natured young bucks from the metal shop became intent on mischief and jumped up on one of the long festival tables where he did the twist.

Corporal George was his name and he was joined by practically everyone in the squadron as joy reigned unrefined.

The bishop, high up on his dais and accompanied by our brass hats, broke into a wide grin of approbation and applauded the forbidden frolic.

He got the joke and loved it.

But whether his joviality was sincere or feigned because he was so deeply in our debt, he rewarded our Dionysian frolic with a hardy round of applause.

We had no bikini or the jovial bishop would probably have modeled it for us.

I was sloshing with beer and badly needed to take a leak so I left the party to find relief somewhere nearby.

Our field head was too far away to make it there so I staggered far enough from the big party that I would not to be noticed and let it fly.

I started back toward the party.

But then something strange came to my ears.

I was just outside our mess tent when I heard the discordant sounds of devilish glee and pitiful whimpering coming from the inside.

Something was wrong in there.

I entered to find Cousin Roy's old Benny boy partners, Brer Bear and Snaggletooth, tormenting a little coolie laborer.

Those two models of moral rectitude were holding that poor, small soul helpless and pricking him with their sharp commando knives.

The reason for their torture was as simple as they were:

It was an open-and-shut case of two dropout ninnies' ignorant attempt to force a poor little captive Buddhist to eat strips of the barbecued sacred Brahma bull's meat.

To give the poor little man his due he had resisted them resolutely and refused to eat that which was at once abominable to him and to his faith.

"Turn that gook loose!" I commanded.

"Who died 'n' lef' YOU in charge, snuffy?" grinned that argumentative Lakeland redneck, Brer Bear.

"What you cock suckers are doin' is way out o' bounds and you know it from th' Nam familiarization lectures."

"He wuz in hyar a-stealin' a bag o' rice," countered Snaggs joyfully, "so wez a-teachin' 'im how ter eat a real man's red meat—"

"You've both been t' th' Nam indoctrination lectures: No saffron flight suits 'n' no insultin' th' Buddhists!"

"Fuck them lect' r' s and FUCK YOU, Delter!" roared Brer Bear pointing his blade at me in a tacit threat.

"No," said I pointing my forty-five right between his puffy eyes, "FUCK YOU is what's playing today:

"I never did like you, Gamble. Now you and Snaggs are gonna die in a few seconds so say 'em if y' know 'em."

"You . . . you aint a-gunna do it, baby boy," countered the now frightened and suddenly sweating Brer Bear, "How you gunna git away wif it, Joe?

"'They gone hang ye fir MURDER!"

"Time for you to learn what we taught Goo-goo Eyes, son:

"There aint no murders in a combat zone, just casualties. Now, make up your tiny little minds whether or not YOU want 'o be a couple o' casualties fast because I'm fixin' t' blow yer shit away 'n' then off the slopey and plant th' gun on this little V. C. who assassinated you."

"We wuz jest havin' some fun wif 'im," the fatally spooked pair whined in their new found capacity of underdogs.

"Well, now I'm havin' MY fun, shit-for-brains," grinned I, "Now, you two Benny boys give this poor little bastard his rice and cut 'im loose!"

They obeyed me now; and their tantalized coolie broke any and all track records in exiting the camp.

"Pay attention and you might learn something, boys," I rubbed it into their thick hides and even thicker heads, "Torture is nothing more than a couple o' lowbrow weaklings like you clowns lording it over a prisoner so they can feel like big shots instead of the sorry ass yard birds you really are."

"We thunk he wuz a enemy agent," grumbled Brer Bear, "We wuz a-tryin' t' make 'im tell us secrets."

The usual flimsy excuse of the torturer.

"When YOU don't speak any gook and he doesn't talk American what kind o' secrets is he gonna tell you?" I sneered down on them, "No, it was like you said in th' first place:

"You were just having some fun with 'im.

"Only problem with that is that we came over here t' be the good guys, children, and th' good guys don't torture."

"Them C. I. A. guys tortures everything they kin lay thar hands on!" was Brer Bear's weak minded apology.

"SO?" I slapped him down, "Are you a marine or a sneak?"

There was much too much of what I've just described in Vietnam then and even more of the same—and worse—in our 21st Century wars of today:

I speak of feasts for the rich notables of the world and their favorites on one side, and torment for the poor on the other.

SHOT DOWN IN A FREE FIRE HOT SPOT

My flight crew and pilots took off for another routine recon flight early, early in the morning as they usually did.

But this hop was not to be business as usual, it was to turn into a major field problem:

After less than an hour up in the blue, the crew chief of that day, Gabe Carrera, felt that all too familiar "thump" against the bird's skin; and jumped out of his seat with a sharp pain in his nether region!

"DAMN!"

At the same time the captain's voice crackled mechanically in Corporal Carrera's flight helmet, "HEY, CREW, ARE YOU OKAY?"

"I'M SHOT IN TH' ASS, SIR!"

"See, Snoopy?" the skipper said to his copilot, "Told y' I saw a muzzle flash down there at maybe four o'clock!

"SHIT! That gook hobo must 'a' got lucky 'n' lobbed one up through th' forward fuel cell!"

"Return t' base, Wimp!" shouted the alarmed copilot.

"No can do! . . . We're leakin' avgas too fuckin' fast, Snoop," was the senior man's concerned reply, "Gotta call home for a new cell 'n' more avgas!

"First things first: How bad is it, crew? . . . You bleedin,' Carrera?"

"No blood, captain, but it hurts!"

"We better get as far as we can from this point of encounter, boys; then find a dry spot in this fuckin' swamp to set this bird down . . .

"Base, we're hit!

"We have damage to forward fuel cell . . . Not enough fuel t' make it home . . . Need gas 'n' new bag mos scosh!"

"Affirmative on your last, chicken hawk," relayed headquarters, "Transmit your coordinates as soon as you set down.

"We are sending you your vital parts and fuel AND a 50 caliber guard bird just in case."

"That's a firm titties on your last, boss man!"

"Hang in there, boys."

Heartened by the realization that they would not be alone in no man's land for more than an hour Captain Wimpy looked for a likely place to land in the vast Cochin China sea of marsh.

He tooled his chopper skillfully to the ground beside a high hammock of trees and radioed his position home.

The nervous trio jumped out of their downed bird like the Marx brothers in one of their frantic comedies and went to work:

Cpl. Carrera and Lt. Snoopy got the cargo deck unbuttoned and out and pulled the ventilated fuel cell in record time.

Capt. Wimpy stood guard with a forty-five caliber submachine gun to watch out for possible enemy patrols.

There was nothing left to do then except to keep an eye out for the enemy and wait for help.

The lecturers on Nam had made it clear that unconventional warriors like the V. C. are always on the move themselves and have no permanent base camps of their own. They just capture an unguarded village then push off when we find out about it: Life on the run.

Therefore, V. C. p. o. w. camps were nonexistent so you might as well fight to the death rather than surrender only to be tortured for your enemy's entertainment and then killed in short order.

It was a big load off our boys' minds when the two relief birds showed up right on time and with no hassles from the enemy patrols.

The repairs were prosecuted post haste, Old Bessy was gassed up faster than she'd ever been before and the boys hightailed it back to base con gusto.

"No shit?" I wondered at my pal's hazardous adventure at the mess that night, "Th' gook shot y' in th' ass? . . . . Where's th' bullet?"

"Yeah.

"It's just lucky we always stow th' rags to clean th' rotor heads under th' crew chief's seat or I'd have a hole where no one wants one 'stead of just a bruise!

"We found th' bullet in th' rags when we took out th' deck BUT th' captain pulled rank on me 'n' kept it for HIS souvenir," was his resentful reply, "Th' fuckin' officers scoff ALL th' trophies of war, Joe."

"That's fucked up."

"No stinkin' shit!" he moaned, "And that's not th' worst of it:

"I got shot in a war zone an' th' colonel won't even put me in f' r a Purple Heart!

"Said we're not at war so he can't put any one in for any war decorations when th' Pentagon says we're not here t'fight a war!"

"Don't y' just love th' Marine Corps?"

"Not so 's y' could notice it right now."

I wonder how our guys who got killed when we "were not at war" might have felt about that?

MOUNTING GUARD IN A COMBAT ZONE

A few days after the big shoot down the butt-bruised hero of that adventure was called upon to walk a post in interior guard.

Being an e4 rank he resented it:

"I," raged Carrera to his captain of the guard that day, "am a corporal e4!

"I'll do my duty as corporal of the guard, but I won't walk no gawdamn post!"

"We got wall-to-wall e4s in this squadron, Carrera," smiled the officer, "Schwandt has seniority over you so he's gonna be our corporal of th' guard. You are going to walk a post."

"I WON'T DO IT, SIR," howled the junior corporal, "I'M AN E4 AND I WON'T TRAMP NO POST!"

"I am ORDERING you to walk guard, Cpl. Carrera," said his captain with deadly calm, "I am telling you, not asking you. "Now, if you want to disobey a direct order, I'll trot you right over to the old man's teepee and you won't have to worry about being a corporal e4 anymore."

Carrera did what he had to do to hang on to those stripes. He put down his head and mumbled, "Aye aye, sir."

As his bad luck would have it poor old Corporal e4 Carrera's post ran right down the path that ran in back of our tent.

"Hey, CORPORAL e4 Carrera," Bob Vick ragged the sore e4, "how come you aint corporal o' th' guard 'stead o' just a lousy sentry?"

"DON'T FUCK WITH ME, SHIT-WIPE!!!" was our boy's furious reply, "DON'T NOBODY FUCK WITH ME T' NIGHT 'R I'LL WASTE ALL OF Y'!!!"

Now, Gabe Carrera was my chopper crew buddy and a good old cartoon pal.

We socialized back in California and my wife, Clara, and I always were sorry that he had a problem wife:

His girl was drop dead beautiful but she had an eighteen carat alcohol addiction.

In addition to that I was genuinely concerned that officers had ganged up and pulled rank to humiliate the poor bastard AGAIN!

But I am a full fledged cheap shot artist and if you ever let a cheap shot artist know that you are a sorehead that makes you too big a target to resist:

I waited until lights out.

Then the time was right for enhanced ridicule plus humiliation laced with psychological torture techniques:

Through the darkness I screamed at the top of my lungs imitating the cry of a great tropical bird, "CARRERA, CARRERA, CARRERA, CARRERA!!!"

"SHUT UP, DELTA, YOU LOUSY CHEAP SHOT SON OF A BITCH!!!" was his rage roar.

"CARRERA-CARRERA-CARRERA-CARRERA-CARRERA-CARRERA-CARRERA-CARRERA!!!"

"DON'T SAY I DIDN'T WARN YOU, DELTA!!!!"

"CARERRA-CARERRA-CARERRA-CARERRA-CARERRA-CARERRA-CARERRA-CARERRA!!!!!"

You get the idea.

Everyone in the area cracked up with the exception of one.

"I'M GONNA KILL YOU, DELTS!!!!"

"CARRERA-CARRERA-CARRERA-CARRERA-CARRERA-CARRERA!!!!"

And so on and on and on through our beloved young corporal's tour of duty.

By that time even Carrera had gotten the joke even though it was on him.

The next night the joke was on me because it was my turn to mount guard in the big Viet swamp.

But I was only a lowly "lance pig" e3 so I did not demand to be the field officer of the day but was content to stand with the rest of the poor folks.

Maybe I better not say "content" considering the large, aggressive mosquito population of America's vacationland and the general tropical malaise there.

"Resigned" is a more accurate way of saying it.

We lugged our rifles, ammo and cartridge belts on over to the guard tent where the cots supplied to the guardsmen were dangerously minus mosquito netting.

But nature was quick to supply the mosquitoes, and it became increasingly more obvious during the passage of my first half hour there that sleep was going to be impossible.

I asked the sergeant of the watch to pick me up at the hanger when it was time to go on because the hanger was sprayed regularly for insects and I might get lucky and get some sleep there. It was no imposition on him because everybody else (including the salty sarge himself) had quickly opted to try it my way as soon as they had heard my plan and felt those stings.

I found a spot in the back near the stored goods and flopped down on the cement hanger deck to get my rest. Cement doesn't make the softest bed in the world but it was beautifully cool laying on it in the hot, humid marshland night and I was soon gratefully, blissfully asleep.

I don't know when he started to work, but I came back to semi-consciousness when I felt a strong tugging at my trouser leg. When I looked down to see what was the matter, I saw the biggest rat I've ever encountered in all of my born days!

This inflated playground of infection was obviously big headed enough to think that he was able to drag me back into the long rows of packing cases where his family lived and have me for a late night snack.

I grabbed my piece and crushed his swelled head with the rifle butt for his impudence.

He let out the disappointed scream of lost ambitions as he died

I kicked his corpse back under a fifty gallon drum after which I went right back to sleep.

Soon after that his family came along to take him back amongst the packing boxes and eat him for their supper in my stead.

A Vietnamese rat is about half the size of a large American pit bull.

All too soon the sergeant woke all of us up to mount interior guard.

The charming Brer Bear and I had adjacent posts on the flight line. We were set there in order to guard against the possible sabotage of our aircraft while the base slept.

We would give the flight line the once around and then sit on a couple of handy chopper struts to hobnob in order to stay awake.

"Whut's up wif YOU, ye misinformed mother fucker?" asked he politely (for a Lakeland rube).

"Y' should 'a' seen th' fuckin' RAT that tried t' carry me off tonight, dumb ass.

"He was just about big enough t' get the job done—"

"Yeah, I hear y'!

"Has yew seen them LIZARDS 'roun' hyar? . . . Them things air DYNOSAURS!"

"Yeah," I chuckled remembering past events in my home tent,

"One o' those eight foot Suzies crawls underneath Bob's bunk every night when it rains lookin' for body heat.

"We call it 'Bob's girlfriend.'"

"THEM BUGS hyar is huge 'n' them reptiles is out o' sight," mused he, "Seem lak th' onliest LITTLE things hyar is th' PEOPLE!"

"LOOK OUT!"

"WHAT TH' FUCK WAS THAT THING?—AN EAGLE?"

A flying creature of monumentally huge proportions with at least a six foot wing-spread had just buzzed us so that a turbulent breeze rushed around our surprised heads from the velocity of its saurian wings.

We got a better look at it as it climbed and the flying giant was a bat the size of a large eagle.

Lopsided Vietnamese animal life is a course of study in itself.

Pleasant dreams, kids.

LITTLE JOE GOES TO THE BIG CITY

Having enjoyed a deeply depressing childhood followed by a stupefying adolescence, I had joined the Marine Corps and gone to war for the expressed purpose of ending my so far miserable life.

I am now happy to report that, after several months of HUK hunting and V. C. chasing, all I had managed to contract was not bullet holes but a tropical ear infection. It would not go away no matter what since we were then in the most tropical part of all the tropics.

The bug was especially painful at night and wouldn't let me sleep.

I voiced my complaint to one of our two ministering naval corpsmen and he gave me an industrial strength prescription antihistomine dose which would let me sleep nights at long last.

Further, our friendly corpsman was kind enough to arrange an appointment for me with the one and only most sadistic and feeble minded navy doctor on our post.

I reported for sick call at the medical tent on the appointed day and hour, and ran into our old Benny boy pal, Brer Bear:

"Whut air YE doin' malingerin' 'roun' this here sick tent, ye misinformed motherfucker?" was his cordial salutation.

"I got an ear infection that won't let me sleep, Lakeland lunkhead," I could not help but smile at the presumption this bottom-of-the-barrel marine, "How 'bout you?"

"Yew writin' a book, jughaid?" was his insolent retort.

"Yeah!

"An' I still got that forty-five, little miss mess tent torture boy, so sing your song while y' still can!"

"Aw . . . I done picked up some kine o' new fangled v. d. which them dumb-ass doctors don' know whut it is.

"THEY calls it nonspecific urethritis an' I calls it a pain in th' ass!"

Poor Lakeland: Leave it to a loser like this one to get AIDS before anyone had heard of it or named it.

"Maybe they'll be able t' cure it," I hoped on his behalf.

"Wall . . . Gud luck t' bof uv us, scrubby-dubby-do!" he grinned.

When it was my turn to be examined our sour-faced little deck-ape lieutenant saw bones poked and prodded and jabbed my sore, sick ear as painfully as he was able untill he got off.

I felt like jumping over the moon, but a marine is not allowed to acknowledge pain.

Then, satisfied that he had tortured a kid who was proscribed even from squirming or letting on that it hurt at all to his heart's delight, the sadistic navy shave-tail admitted the obvious:

He didn't know what this exotic infection was.

His recommendation was that I be sent to Saigon where there were rumored to be senior medicos who actually knew their asses from a hole in the ground.

"Gud luck . . ." as Brer Bear had put it.

The up-side to my appointment with Navy Lieutenant Bozo the clown was that he prescribed enough dope to let me sleep nights.

Our big going-to-Saigon day started early like every day in the military begins.

We dragged ourselves down to the flight line before dawn.

The pilots showed up and pre-flight inspected the ship.

We all piled in and flew to Saigon.

It must have been too dark for the enemy to see as yet so we weren't even fired upon this time and that made it a red letter day in the delta.

Our hop was blissfully uneventful and the captain gave us an in flight travel log:

"See that burnt out spot down there?

"That's what's left o' Bein Hoa where they pulled their Mayday Offensive 'n' we burned 'em out."

And an hour later:

'That charred patch o' terrain below us right now used t' be Can Tho where they pulled that Fourth of July Offensive 'n' guess what?"

"We burned th' ville," was our safe guess.

"Spot on!" complemented his co.

"All in all we were very offensive." smiled the skipper.

We all laughed on cue.

A little while later:

"And here is our destination, troops: Saigon, world famous home of th' bicycle bombers!"

Saigon was a fairly large city for such a tiny country and stretched out for miles below us.

Before landing the skipper treated us to an aerial side jaunt around the recently bombed presidential palace whence the iron clawed Dragon Lady ruled through her signal tools—torture and terror.

"Some commie hot shot flew a small craft under the nationalist's radar 'n' bombed Mme. Ngo's home torture chamber," remarked the cap admiringly.

"Anything for a laugh with those fuckin' Viet Cong wing jockeys!"

We lit at last and headed for our quarters in a posh, formerly French colonial hotel now housing neo-colonial American military service personnel.

"It's siesta time right now," instructed our duty n. c. o. host, "and we advise all Americans to stay off the streets during th' siesta. There are quite a few murders and bombings at that time so it's a whole lot safer to just lay low, men."

So we took a rest and examined the hotel's fanciful accoutrements.

This opulent accommodation was pure Franco posh right down to the bidet fitted commodes.

When the local authority thought that we might venture outside again we went across the street to a bistro for a first rate meal.

It was a tiptop nosh from soup to nuts.

As we boarded a cab for a close up look at the dread Mme. Ngo's palace of horrors we were fit to burst with rich, Frenchicfied up town chow.

We had no sooner pulled away from the curb than the café we had patronized only seconds earlier went up in flames in the deafening roar of high explosive fury.

The plate glass window we had looked out of a minute or two ago along with most of the restaurant's front wall and all of the furnishings and people inside blew past the rear of our taxi and all over the opposite side of the street cross the street in flaming chards and burning, bloody shredded pulp.

"Hot dang!" gasped Brer Bear, "That-thar could o' jest been US!"

"I got no luck at all," groused death wish Delta.

"Speak fir yore own self, Crazy Joe!" scolded Lakeland hotly, "Maybe YOU wants ter git kilt, but not me!"

We got to the palace without further misadventure because our driver was not one of those (and there were many) who would bring American service men to a Viet Cong slum and park them there and run leaving our comrades to be slaughtered by their blood foemen—AND girls.

The residence was about middle sized as the ornate palaces of rulers go.

Toward the rear of that pile was what had once been a dome but was now a roofless crater thanks to that resourceful rogue Viet Cong bomber.

The guards around the palace were nervous and not particularly friendly. For those reasons we did not ask them for a guided tour.

One might have been arranged because when unpopular rulers are bombed they always hightail it from the bombed residence to someplace they think might be a safer venue for them to forge heavier chains for the masses they oppress in secret.

Not far away from the Dragon Lady's torture town house were the notorious Tiger Cages.

This dreaded prison was the ultimate destination of any and all suspected V. C. who had been unlucky enough to survive their initial interrogators' best efforts to make them squeal or make them corpses.

We were able to approach this tenth pit of hell for a small bribe to the prison guards:

The luckless culprits imprisoned there were displayed beneath ground level beneath an iron grate at the feet of their captors. Those Francophile gentlemen towered over the burnt and mutilated bodies of their victims below who mourned their cruel fate awash in subterranean seepage from the sewers and their own blood and excrement.

Periodically, the laughing guard officers would don protective gloves to armor their own dainty hands from harm and throw caustic lye down through the grating upon their agonized tormented their captives screaming below ground level.

This inhumane practice etched striped burns in the naked flesh of their mutilated writhing, screaming victims beneath the grate. That's why they are called a Tiger Cages:

Because the imps in uniform above etched excruciating stripes into the naked flesh of the inmates in hell.

"Haint that somethin,'" gaped the admiring Brer Bear, "I shore do wisht that I hat that kine o' POWER.

"I'd give it ter them gosh dern slopies fir record!!!"

"You would, you lard-ass little knuckle dragger!

This is a revolting practice from th' dark ages," I berated the goon.

"Shit howdy, Crazy Joe!" he grumbled, "Why duz you alus gotta be such a goody two shoes ball buster?

"Don' chew never-ever jus' relax 'n' have some fuckin' fun?"

"We have different ideas about how t' relax I guess, Dudley dumb shit."

That's the history of torture and torturers in a nut case:

Torture fans are amoral piss ants trying to play god; and rubbing it in by humiliating their captive adversaries.

We had just witnessed the practice of the most naked and indefensible epitome of inhuman insanity imaginable.

It had grabbed us both in its vice-like grip of morbid fascination.

WE had witnessed the primitive and devilish desire of one man to be the unquestioned master of his fellow men.

It was a powerful and riveting experience.

We had personally seen the way that this perverse desire had driven these "civilized" men back and back and further back into the id state of a power crazed brute. That is how and why war brings out the spirit of the Inquisition in humankind's baser types.

It certainly had forced Lakeland into its thrall.

Perhaps this plague is endemic for we witness its resurgence every time that we sink low enough to employ war as a simple solution to a host of complex problems. And that is the exact reason why our problems are never solved:

One war generates the next war which gives birth to the next and so on ad infinitum.

Militarists and war their warmongering industries, our home grown domestic enemies, are expert propagandists.

They excel in the field of generating hatred and directing it outward against the foreign "enemy" whose wealth and resources they want to steal in order to power the next "righteous war" because we're the "good guys."

These imperialists—our most dangerous enemies whose unquenchable greed and bloodlust gnaws away at the vitals of our own sick society—will make it ever weaker until our sleeping people arise to expel their fascist perversion of "Amerika," in order to bring about a reborn democratic America that we may attain a new and higher level of civilization.

I speak of an as yet undreamed of zenith of civilized existence never yet achieved in any quarter other than those war weary defunct European empires who have at long, long last learned the painful lesson of the price of their own arrogance.

And those ex empires learned it the hard way when they saw their own capital cities reduced to smoldering heaps of rubble.

(Even then the slow learning and empire obsessed and needy Brits are even now content to be tag-along as junior partner aggressors in Wimp II 's Iraqi oil grab folly and further imperial adventure schemes.).

We tore ourselves away from the rancid scene of the tiger cages after Brer Bear had asked both humbly and repeatedly to be allowed to throw some lye on the burning prisoners below.

Unfortunately for him the required bribe level was too high; he was broke due to his free-spending habits.

And—predictably—I had refused to lend him any lye throwing money.

When we pulled up in front of our hotel barracks the debris of our exploded café had already been cleared away and carpenters, glaziers and masons were hard at work repairing the considerable damages to the building.

"Heavy!," we exclaimed.

"Oh, yeah, babies," grinned our loyalist cabby, "In Saigon City we no fuck around, g. i."

Back at the hotel we walked through the Rococo stone arcades designed to keep the heat off of the former European taskmasters of that land. It was beautifully shaded in there and actually cooler than most places in Nam as a whole.

The natives of Saigon make scant secret about their feelings toward the hated round eyes and if looks could kill I wouldn't be writing this now.

Most of the natives we passed on the streets and in the arcades of Saigon took care not to look us directly in the eye; but those among them who did showed me the eye of the tiger burning with a murderous hatred of the foreign devil.

We made it to our doctors' appointments right on time to learn that the medics there did not know any more about what was wrong with us than their juniors in the field had known.

Those geniuses phoned our colonel at the front to say that they wanted to send us to Tokyo where other learned physicians might evaluate our conditions and come up with more of the same bull shit.

Zeus on high was not buying any of their verbal soft soap and fertilizer:

"YOU FULL O' SHIT CROAKERS SEND MY BOYS BACK HERE INSTANTER!!!!

"I'M DOWN HERE IN A RED HOT WAR ZONE TRYING T' FIGHT A WAR AND YOU SISSIES 'RE GONNA TAKE AWAY MY MARINES.THAT HAVEN'T EVEN YET BEEN SHOT UP YET?

"NOT HARDLY!!!"

(Everybody had learned to talk while watching GUN SMOKE in those early sixties days.)

"Can't you spare these two men, colonel?"

"DON'T YOU KNOW WHAT THE WORD 'NO' MEANS?

"NOT THOSE TWO—THEY'RE TWO O' MY CRAZIEST!

"NOW, YOU SEND 'EM BACK HERE ON TH' HUMP!!!"

And back to Soc Trang we went.

Nor were we sorry about that for from what we had seen it was a hell of a lot safer in our "RED HOT WAR ZONE" than it was in the "civilized" city of Saigon.

NEW FLASHBACKS FOR OLD

The funny thing about being in a do or die combat hot spot is that you don't have flashbacks about Nam while you are in Nam:

You flash to Parris Island. It's like having a nightmare about another nightmare while struggling through your present nightmare.

You get to the Marine Corps Recruit Training Depot and spend your first night in some sort of receiving barracks. Then early, early, EARLY at the next dawn of day you are awakened by the folks who are to be your ever loving drill instructors on the island of the damned.

With a generous helping of oaths and blows these new friends and kindhearted teachers drive you down to the pavement outside the barracks like so many cattle to the slaughtyer

AWRIGHT, LADIES, I WANT TO SEE THREE GAWDAMN ROWS O' CORN STANDIN' TALL RIGHT HERE IN FRONT O' ME," roars the head man, "WHUT 'RE YOU WAITIN' ON, YOU MIS'ABLE SHIT-COOLIES?

"I DON' MEAN SOMETIME NEX' YEAR, I MEAN NOW NOWNOWNOW NOW!!!"

Everyone scampers into three frightened "ROWS O' CORN" ranks.

"MY NAME IS ACTING GUNNERY SERGEANT ANTHRAX AND I WILL BE YOUR FIRST SENIOR DRILL INSTRUCTOR UNTIL YOU FUCK UP AND I SET YER ASS BACK ANYWAYS . . .

"RECRUITS, MORE THAN A MOTHER FUCKIN' THIRD O' YOU SWEET LI' L' PANSY-ASS MOMMA'S LITTLE GIRLS AINT A-GUNNA MAKE IT THROUGH PARRIS ISLAND MARINE CORPS BOOT CAMP:

YOU DON'T PACK TH' GEAR—YOU AINT MAN ENOUGH—YOU SHIT MAGGOTS AND Y' DON'T HAVE WHUT IT TAKES T' BE A MARINE.

"AND WHEN I FINDS OUT WHO Y' ARE I'M GONNA SHIT CAN YOU OUT O' MY MARINE CORPS!!!"

After this warm welcome your hard case n. c. o. i. c. begins to run you through the P. I. course of sprouts.

There is a whole bunch of getting up before dawn and running three miles and sometimes more in many and many a grueling lap around the 2nd battalion p. t. field; and other times around and around and around one stop sign just to piss you off and teach you something about life's hopeless futility.

That was if you had not already spotted life's sarcastic irony in the harsh reality of existing by grit and determination through the grind this hard venue.

Then after three pull-ups you are graciously allowed to:

"MARCH INTO CHOW AT ATTENTION" in order to wolf down breakfast in fifteen minutes, "AND FIFTEEN MINUTES ONLY!

"I EATS NOW AN' CHEWS LATER, RECRUITS!" is your "damn idiot's" austere stern caveat.

By now you have been issued your technical ordinance weapon and full combat 782 gear in which and with which you run around the island at double time march till your time there is up.

There are daily classes on the t. o. weapon, the Browning automatic rifle, the 45 caliber service automatic pistol and lots of other field ordinance goodies.

I'm a history nut so the classes on Marine Corps history, mission and tradition suited me best.

There were grueling hours on the physical training field which were conducted by a particularly sadistic p. t.—or p. t.—instructor:

"OUR FIRST EXERCISE WILL BE PUSHUPS—TEN OF 'EM—ALL THE WAY UP AND ALL TH' WAY DOWN: IF YOU DO NOT DO THEM CORRECTLY WE WILL START ALL OVER!"

These babies had a special and skillful way of conducting a ball busting dance macabre.

"PRIVATE VOLPE DID NOT GO ALL THE WAY DOWN FOR THAT ONE," was the habitual remonstrance, "WE'LL START ALL OVER:

"ONE!"

"ONE, SIR!!!"

"NOW PRIVATE PEST IS DOPING OFF ON US:

"ONE!"

"ONE, SIR!"

We probably did ten thousand pushups to come at last, sweating, gasping for air and deeply sore in every sinew of our bodies, to the perfect ten pushups.

All of that was followed by a shower back at the squad bay and—just in case we had gotten soft in the shower—more p. t. with our beloved drill instructor.

His exercises were embellished with such Parris Island niceties as "watching television."

"D' YOU LAK T' WATCH TELEVISION, RECRUIT?"

"YES, SIR!" was the reply of the uninitiated innocent.

(Oh, never, never tell these good sports that you like anything!)

"THEN GIT IN TH' PUSHUP POSITION ONLY WITH YORE ELBOWS SUPPORTIN' TH' WEIGHT OF YORE BODY 'N' YER HANDS CLAMPED BEHIND YER EARS ON YER NECK!"

"YES . . . SIR?"

"NOW YOU STAY THAT WAY TILL I TELL YOU T' STOP WATCHIN' TELEVISION!"

That torture test continues for about half an hour of strain and pain until the d. i. stops it; or, as is often the case, the boot passes out.

There are frequent disciplinary romps in the squad bay in which when the d. i. covers the head of a recruit in disfavor and bangs on that metal utensil loudly and with all his might with his swagger stick until he isn't mad anymore.

There is a peaceful little creek out near the rifle range notorious in the annals of boot camp overreaction for The Ribbon Creek Incident:

An unacceptable percentage of A.S.S. McCool's platoon had failed to qualify as survival swimmers.

Ribbon Creek was swollen and treacherous due to a hurricane that had just blown through.

The acting staff sergeant was furious with the boys' failure to qualify at any test of strength.

He had been drinking that night and he marched his swimming non quals out there for a dip.

Predictably, everything had gone wrong.

McCool was a strong, young buck and managed to pull most of his boys out of the storm-swollen current to safety, but two of the boys had died of drowning.

Their d. i. was busted down to corporal and the public hew and cry was so loud that Congress established an "Observation Unit" to be stationed on Parris Island to look for any and all evidence of overboard hazing and acts of wanton cruelty.

Just as our greeter to the recruit depot had foretold, after a while people do start dropping out:

Plowright, he kid with whom I had made the trip up to Parris Island by bus, had started crying when a d. i. was just screaming in his face and not even hitting him.

He was immediately sent to the psychiatric observation unit for diagnosis.

Parris Island is the easiest place in the world to escape if you are so inclined. For all you need do is to tell the psychiatrist that your drill instructor is picking on you.

Marines are the first attack wave in a war and if you can't take the rough stuff they want to know that you are a luxury they can't afford in boot camp before you can fall apart where the hop is rocking with flying lead and you can blow an entire field problem for your whole unit.

Recruit Plowright was examined.

The needle "track" marks where he had been in the habit of injecting heroin in civilian life were discovered; it was deemed that he was not marine material and off he went to shoot some more horse in civilian life.

Vendi was so gung ho that he was "digging 'em in" and fractured both of his heels in his ardor.

And away he went out of the corps.

Siskin was too inclined to sulk and not fast moving enough to suit the powers that be so he was packed off to the motivation platoon in an arcane installation on the rifle range known as the special training unit.

He had been "set back!"

Being set back was not only a mark of disgrace, but it also meant that you would have to spend more time being hard-assed by the goons in charge of you on Parris Island.

Being set back in your course of training was a form of humiliation which the drill instructors often and successfully used as a threat over the recruits to get more out of us.

Then doom struck all of us in our training series and we all caught The Parris Island Special, a particularly debilitating strain of influenza.

As a result of that menace a little kid named Kenesy and I failed the two week strength test and were promptly set back to strength and hospital platoon at s. t. u.

Now we—like poor old Siskin—were the "maggots in disgrace!"

So we would have to try ten times as hard as the rest of the boots back main side to get back up to snuff so that we might go back there to finish the course and get the hell off of this island of the damned.

There were three platoons at the special training unit:

Strength and hospital which sported a far more compassionate regime and d. i. than the others (or yet the main side series). All that our d. i. out there was concerned with was building the recruit up physically and contributing to his conditioning until he was healthy enough to complete his rigorous ordeal back in a main side training series.

Fat mans' platoon was more gut-slamming because the task was harder for those drill instructors because they had to get enough lard off of the obese recruit to render him fit to complete main side training.

The fat men were treated like animals.

And the guys in motivation platoon were treated worse than either of the first two because they were judged to be undisciplined which was a definite taboo in Uncle Sam's Misguided Children.

One kid in motivation was singled out by the mighty powers there anjd condemned by them never to make it off the island with the honor of graduating and becoming a marine.

They had decided to keep him in motivation platoon until he broke down and begged the shrink to release him or until the doctors mustered him out themselves.

This horrifying and dolorous example steeled the resolve in the rest of us to fight our way back through this harsh regimen to the 1st Battalion parade field and there to wear our newly awarded Marine Corps emblems with pride on Graduation Day.

One bleak, windswept, drizzling afternoon when we were working out of doors on the strength platoon wash racks Brother Kensey faced me with a wild look in his hurt young eyes filled with fear and uncertainty and said in his confusion:

"What must we do, big daddy?"

"Persevere, son, we must persevere at all costs," was my advice to the youngster.

Then I told him what perseverance was, and we both agreed that it was the only way out of this fix.

Training schedules were double hard in our strength and hospital platoon; but with the help and good advice of our d. i. we were able to persevere, pass the test and get back into another main side platoon.

We stood tall and proud when our d. i. pinned our Marine emblems on our uniforms as we faced Iron Mike and Boulevard de France and we were truly marines at last.

On the evening and after graduation, the darling A. S. S. Fat Bones called me into his office for some final words of valediction:

"PRIVATE DELTA, I NEVER DIDN'T NEVER LIKE YOU 'N' I STILL DON'T LIKE YOU 'N' I DON'T THINK YOU ARE A MARINE OR ARE EVER GUNNA BE A MARINE:

SO NOW I'M A-GUNNA SET YOU BACK!!!"

"I don't think you can do that after I have graduated, sergeant fat ass," I answered able to stand up to the titanic bully on my hind legs at last, "But just in case you can and do:

"I would advise you never to go t' sleep on Parris Island again."

"WHUT CHEW GONER DO IF I DOES, DISREPECKFUL PUNK?" roared Bonsey furiously.

"You'll never wake up because my bayonet will be stuck through your heart when they find your fat, dead body in th' mornin'."

A crooked smile brightened his grim death mask of a face that had scarcely ever smiled in all its days as it suddenly dawned on him that I had become his kind of homicidal maniac while undergoing the rigors of boot training.

Fat Bones stuck out that hard recruit pounding paw to shake

"Well, well, WELL, Little Joe!

"Maybe we done turnt you inta a marine after all."

Too much is enough and here is a flashback from the actual killing fields rather than the training to kill boot camp:

Do you remember how mom, dad and little brothers and sisters used to watch the Technicolor war with its blood, screams and torn, burned and mutilated body parts flying?

Remember how those scenes that brought the final tortured moments of the dead and dying right into their living rooms and made them see war for what it is?

Remember how that experience had galvanized our entire population against the Viet-war and how it helped to ultimately stay the carnage there and on our campuses?

The home folks got a good visual idea of the rampant slaughter brought forth through imperialist hubris. But it wasn't really yet a complete picture.

For a good look at war's face you had to be in it over there—feeling the heat and smelling the stink and seeing your pals and native innocent bystanders buy the farm in front of your eyes.

And, above all, you had to wonder who was going to be next in that Grim Reaper's great harvest home.

You?

Your pals?

The old?

The weak?

The women?

The helpless?

But never the bishop or the Ngos or L. B. J. OR McNamara.

Never the ones who fan the flame of war.

No, never anyone on a pedestal.

("K" Street and the Pentagon and the imperialists for corruption of today have realized that colonial wars and full news disclosure don't mix.

In his inexcusable Iraq aggression the White House top jump-the-gun, George "Wimp II" Bush, was sure to hide the dark side of his folly from the rude gaze of the public.

The only film that got back from Iraq was doctored a la Nazi WWII propaganda flicks because the only reports out of there were from "embedded" pro-war Pentagon plant reporters

That was a politic way of saying bare faced liars.

And Iraq drags on.

But finally a brave young man with a camera at the Abu Garib torture camp made sure that Wimp II AND his goofy gaggle of neocon Nazis got caught in the act with their knickers at half mast.

Torture camp photos surfaced and had leaked out to blow out the sneaky bubble boy's cover.)

Back to our dirty little war in Nam:

It was another hot, oppressive day in the Mekong Delta.

Tent city and the people therein including yours truly were sweltering.

Our bird with its two pilots and flight crew had gone up early in the morning on some kind of rescue hop; and I was laying around in our sweat box of a tent waiting for their return.

I must have dozed off because when I came to my senses it was no longer early morning but early afternoon and Old Bessie was back and locked and chocked out there on the flight line.

But for some unknown reason her cargo bay was all buttoned up.

"What gives?" I wondered in puzzlement, "This never happens ... The birds are always open when they're on th' mat ..."

I shuffled toward our aircraft suspecting that there must be some kind of a mess in the cargo hold that I would be expected to clean up.

I had to check and see.

I was close to the cargo hatch now, but something had made me pause and slow down.

Maybe it was an indefinable hint of burning flesh and zoological corruption hanging over me in the heavy, humid and oppressive air.

What was that odeor that was creeping stealthily and sickeningly into my nostrils?

Or it may have been muffled, almost indistinguishable sounds which were emanating from within the secured hull of our airship.

I stood dead still in my tracks for a second—suspended in time.

But why?

"Enough of this woolgathering nonsense!" I commanded myself.

I threw open the cargo bay hatch with a flourish.

Inside the crew-space was a preview of hell:

A small multitude of slight and tiny people, or what was left of them, all of them burned, most of them mutilated, dismembered and awfully distorted were moaning their death pangs because they no longer had the strength left to cry out.

Disfigured and charred young mothers in an advanced state of shock clasped their dead babies to breasts that would never again be milked because these young mothers were soon to join their poor little children on the other side as well.

Their neighbors—over a dozen expiring semi-corpses—lay racked with agony and experiencing fits of gasping for breath on the crew-space deck and writhing awash in their own vomit and excrement.

I'd seen it all but this was the capper and even I went pale.

"PUTTON OP DOT FUCKIN' CARGO HATCH BEFORE ZOMPODY ZEES VOT'S IN THERE, TELTA YOU STUPID LOAFER!" raged one of our ex Nazi pro war zealots, Sgt. Doomkopf.

"Sgt. Dummy" as we all called him had been riding with my senior crew chief on today's hop.

"I take my orders from Gunny Burns, Dummy," said I for his information.

On the odd occasion Gunnery Sergeant Burns, my boss crew chief let Dummy ride along with him.

Occasions did not get any odder than flights with psycho boy Doomkopf aboard!

"UNT TON'T LOOK ZOO FUCKIN' KVEEZY OFFER A BUNCH UF KOTDAMN GOOKS!!!

"GOTT TAM IT:

"I SHOOT ZIXTEEN UF DEM COCK SUCKERS DEAD TODAY MIENZELF!

"UNT I CARVE DEM NOTCHES IN MIEN RIFLE PUTT PEECAUSE I AM PROUD UF VOT I DONE!!!

"ZOO TON'T GO GA-GA OFFER NO V. C. CARPAGE LIKE DEM!!!"

"Let th' poor little bastard be, Nazi-boy," said Gunny Burns catching up with the wrathful wailer, "It's a raw sight.

"Toss yer waffles if y' gotta, kid—I know I did."

"No . . . no . . . I'm . . . okay, boss," lied I.

"Good boy!

"There was an Air Force defoliation Napalm bombing just north o' here 'n' these poor slobs and their village just happened to be in th' target area.

"What a way t' go!"

"We're gonna fly 'em back t' were there's a real hospital . . . But most of 'em won't make it.

"Old Bessy's all greased up 'n' ready t' go—y' gotta keep Old Dummy busy or he gets in trouble.

"Well, boys, here come th' pilots so all you have t' do, Delts is to pull th' chocks 'n' taxi us out.

"I an gonna get DRUNK TONIGHT and I'd advise you to do the same, son!"

"Yes, sir!"

I taxied her out and watched her climb without much hope for those poor villagers.

When she came back I hosed out the befouled crew-space and tried to forget what I had seen there.

But neither I nor anyone else was ever able to clean up the Viet-war.

Here's another pretty little vignette for you to take to bed with you for pleasant dreams:

Remember our little dapper Dan Vietnamese base barber who had given us of the air marines so much solace?

You won't soon forget him when I tell you of that gentle old soul's fate.

One early morning when the m. p and the truck driver were on the way to town for a water run to be shot at for their trouble he stopped long enough to radio in about something he had found on the way:

The little old barber's ten-speed was propped up in the middle of the road.

The little barber's bloodstained and severed hands were grasping the bicycle's hand grips

The cycle's seat had been removed so that the poor old soul's murderers were able stick the his still quite neatly groomed severed head on the bar which had once supported that seat.

But only the V. C. and The Buddha know where the rest of his body lay.

Oh, those mad Viet Cong wags!

They had bicycle bombed everyone and everything in sight and they'd wrecked the presidential palace.

They always and habitually had run a flock of innocent bystanders out between our fire and theirs to be shot down in cold blood in order to score a propaganda victory off of us,

They had destroyed the entire adult male population of Vietnam for two generations.

But their latest macabre merry prank was a grisly gambol mixed with mystery:

What had become of our little barber's torso, arms and legs?

Only our invisible enemy and Infinity knew the answer.